MARBLEHEAD BOAT NAMES

SECOND EDITION

By Susan Cairns Fischer

MARBLEHEAD BOAT NAMES

Published by Lighthouse Publishing,
151 Atlantic Avenue, Marblehead, MA 01945

Susan Fischer
Author

Sarah Fischer
Editor

Francesca Mastromarino
fmmastromarino@gmail.com
Cover Art

ISBN 978-0-9641013-1-9
Second Edition
Printed in the United States of America

To purchase additional copies of this book, visit:
www.marbleheadboatnames.com

ACKNOWLEDGEMENTS

Thank you to all of the Marblehead waters boat owners for your contributions, which made this book possible!

Thank you to my family- Jack, Sarah and Kiley, for your extremely valuable assistance and support!

WARNING – DISCLAIMER

This book is designed to be both informative and entertaining. Every effort has been made to ensure that the information in this book is as accurate and complete as possible. However, there may be mistakes both typographical and in content.

The research for this book was conducted during the summer of 2014. The information received was compiled and then combined with the information that was presented in the first edition of MARBLEHEAD BOAT NAMES. Each contributor was asked to provide their boat's name, type, length, and true story behind the name.

The story for each boat was obtained from either the boat's owner or relative. If the story provided was a direct quote, it will appear in quotations. To protect the privacy of each boat owner, full names were omitted from this book.

As stated above, this book is designed to be both informative and entertaining. Please sit back, relax, read and enjoy!

MARBLEHEAD AND ITS WATERS

Originally part of Salem until it's incorporation as a town in 1649, Marblehead, Massachusetts is located 17 miles north of Boston. This beautiful, year-round seacoast community with its picturesque harbor, is well known as the 'yachting capital of America'. Marblehead is also infamous for being the 'birthplace of the American Navy'.

The owners of the moorings residing in the waters of Marblehead are very fortunate, as moorings can be hard to come by. There is currently an 18+ year wait to obtain a mooring in Marblehead Harbor!

During the summers, the waters of Marblehead fill up with a wide assortment of boats. It is fun to look at the different boat names and try to guess what they mean. This book tells you what hundreds of these names really mean!

Marblehead Waters
Mooring Zones Chartlet

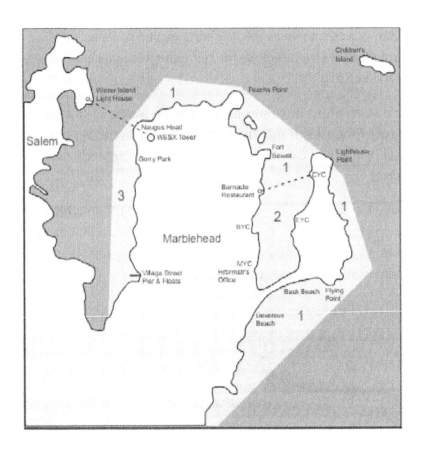

Notes: Not to scale. Not to be used for navigation.
2001 Manual for Marblehead Waters

MARBLEHEAD BOATS

AND

THE REAL STORIES BEHIND THEIR NAMES

A ———

ABALASH (21' AQUASPORT) "The boat is named after my three daughters, Abigail, Alyssa and Ashley."

ABASHI (24' MAKO) "Captains Courageous."

ABERLOUR (31' ERICSON INDEPENDENCE CUTTER) "Aberlour is designed by acclaimed naval architect Bruce King as a classic cruiser. Only 69 hulls were made between 1978-1981. Aberlour is hull #41. The boat is named for one of the owner's favorite Highland single malt Scotch whiskeys, which is in turn named for where it's distilled in Aberlour, Scotland. Aberlour A'Bunadh, matured at cask strength in Spanish Oloroso cask butts, is among the finest and rarest of the scotch, just like Aberlour the classic sailboat that plies Marblehead waters and beyond."

ACHIEVER (36' FRERS) "The previous owner was active in Junior Achievement. That suggested the name."

ADJO (13' WHALER) "The name represents both sons, Adam and Josh."

ADVENTURE (19' O'DAY MARINER) "Because life is one big adventure!"

AEOLUS (31' BERTRAM) "Aeolus was named by my father who favors the Greek classics. Aeolus was a Greek god from Homer's <u>Odyssey</u> and is known as the keeper of the wind. It is an ironic name for a power boat."

AEROPHILIA (33' FRERS) "The draft of wind."

AFRICA (44' SAIL) "Another Fricken Racer I Can't Afford."

AFTER FIVE (22' O'DAY) "This boat was named by the previous owner."

AFTER YOU (20 REGAL) "Every time someone asks me the name of my boat I say, 'I named it after you!' It's always good for a few laughs."

AFTON (20' CORINTHIAN) "Afton is a Scottish river immortalized in poem and song. I got the inspiration when I saw a shop in La Jolla, CA named Afton. It says peace, serenity and gentleness."

AHI (21' BOSTON WHALER) "A number of years ago when fishing in Hawaii, I hooked up with a big yellowfin tuna. The yellowfin tuna is called 'Ahi' in the islands. This means 'ball of fire', which I consider a very appropriate name."

AIR APPARENT (40' J) "All our previous boats were named Airborne, after the William F. Buckley book by the same name. When we bought the J40, it was the 'heir apparent' to the previous boats. Apparent because we weren't sure if it would be the last in line. Air Apparent was the play on words used to remind ourselves that there still could be one more boat. Isn't there always 'one more boat' to think about?"

AIR TRACKS (25' CAPE DORY) "Air tracks are a piece of apparatus built by my company and used to teach physics in college. It seemed like a provocative name for a sailboat."

AIRWAVE (26' PEARSON) "My husband's career is in radio news. Since the Pearson needs air to fill her sails and carry her over the waves, the connection between career and boat seemed natural."

AJA (29' C&C) "The yacht AJA was named after my wife Anne, children Jesse and Jenna, and myself, Alan. The group Steely Dan also had an album and song named AJA. My wife and I were partial towards Steely Dan. So goes the name!"

ALETHEA (13' WIDGEON) "She is named after our daughter, Alethea, whose name was inspired in part by a beautiful white boat from the Mystic, Connecticut area. That boat itself had been named after the owner's wife, Alethea."

ALLEGRO SEMPLICITA (10.5 meters J105) "My father's racing boats were all called 'Allegro', but when he retired from racing he named his cruising boat 'Allegro Vivace', still fast but for the fun of it. When he became ill, his cruising boat fell into disrepair and we encouraged him to down size and add simplicity.... 'allegro semplicita'....fast with simplicity. Sadly he never sailed on the new boat so named as his health deteriorated beyond his ability to do so, but his legacy lives on."

ALLEGRO VIVACE (37.5 J) "Allegro and vivace are musical terms. Allegro means fast and vivace means lively, which of course is Italian. The name fits the boat."

ALTERED STATES (30' S-2) "Me!"

AMERICAN ANTHEM (35' 1938 SPARKMAN & STEVENS SLOOP) "She was originally built for Percival Chubb, of the

Chubb Insurance Company, and sailed in the Long Island Sound area. Her names have included TOPGALLANT, AKBAR and ARION. This is our first wooden vessel and the first worthy of the title 'Yacht'. We wanted a name that would fit her origins, her history, and her classic lines. The unanimous choice, no discussions required, appears on the transom, AMERICAN ANTHEM. A classic name for a very special yacht. (P.S. The tender for this boat is O SAY---)"

AMERICAN FLYER (25' CATALINA) "I am a captain for American Airlines. Therefore it follows that I am a flyer and work for American. Plus, it's a takeoff on western flyer bikes (from the old days), eastern flyer sleds, etc..."

ANANDA (44' CHERUBINI) "My Cherubini 44' came with the name 'Afrita', Arabic for demon woman. That didn't feel right for such a graceful, beautiful boat. So, we came up with 'Ananda', Hindi for pure bliss and joy which is what Ananda has been for me for the past 18 years. Years after the name change I learned that Ananda was The Buddha's first cousin and his attendant after The Buddha's enlightenment. Yet another wonderful meaning for the boat's name."

ANANEA (36' S2 LEVIN) "Buddha, god of ultimate happiness."

ANDIAMO (28' CUSTOM CUTTER) "This is Italian for, 'Let's go!'"

ANDREA SEA (28' ERICSON) "My wife's middle initial is C=SEA." (The wife's first name is Andrea.)

ANDROMEDA (38' C&C) "Named for Andromeda, daughter of Cassiopeia, who was consigned to drown chained to a rock, by jealous Greek goddesses. Pursues, god of the sea, happened by and fell in love with her. Because she was very beautiful, he saved her. We always felt it would be a lucky name for a boat."

ANNIE (24' A. BRENDZE WOODEN SLOOP) "In 1980, we attended ANNIE's christening at the Arundel Yacht Yard in Kennebunkport without ever knowing we'd own her five years later. ANNIE's builder, Arthur Brendze, explained her name in a Marblehead Reporter article written by Marshall Frederics: '…Later, over chicken pate and punch, Arthur explained the name. 'Because she's an orphan, you see. Whoever buys her may want to change her name and to change a boat's name is considered bad luck by many boatsmen. Orphans, however, often change their names when they're adopted. In this case, it won't be bad luck.'"

ANTICIPATION (30' SABRE) "As a salesman, I have always thought that one should always 'Anticipate' and never assume. I also had a J24 with a not-so-dependable outboard. My goal was to someday get a 30 footer with an inboard. While I always anticipated, it was my daughter who finally said, 'Just buy it!'"

ANTIDOTE (17' BOSTON WHALER) "Going off for a quick trip in this boat clears my mind from the worries and problems. It is my 'antidote' for those down times, and lifts my spirit."

APPLEGARTH (36' CAPE DORY CUTTER) "Applegarth, according to legend, is where Merlin retired from the court of Camelot. 'Garth' is Welch for home or cottage. 'Apple' referred to an orchard. After serving Arthur until he was crowned, Merlin desired a simpler life and moves away from the castle to a cottage in the orchards named Applegarth. (There he met Numive, but that's another legend for another boat someday.)"

AQUADUCK (20' AQUASPORT) "I have run several sports outings with friends over the years with a 'Duck' theme. When I bought this boat a good friend suggested the name 'Aquaduck'. It was appropriate and nothing else appealed to me. So for the last 30 years, the Aquaduck has provided my family and friends a lot of on-water fun times."

AQUITAINE (16' MAKO) "Region of France (land of waters)."

ARBELLA (40' TAYLOR) "ARBELLA is named after the first ship from England bearing settlers to Salem. She was renamed for the ranking woman on the passage, Lady Arbella Jones. Salem has a street, a drum corps and a yarn shop named after her. Until destroyed, Salem had a ¾ replica. (My use of the name predates the insurance company Arbella.)"

ARCADIAN (22' SAILMASTER) "Often not capitalized: a person who lives a simple quiet life. I've also heard it mean 'Utopia' in modern poetry. -or- endless summers, joyous times, playful and non-reality based living (Greek mythology) D: All of the above."

ARCO IRIS (29' J) "Arco iris = Spanish for rainbow = a great J boat!"

ARGONAUTA (32' PEARSON) "As frequent vacationers in Captive, Florida, my wife, Rebecca, was introduced to Anne Morrow Lindbergh's book <u>Gift from the Sea</u> in 1996, the same year we purchased a 1981 32' Pearson sloop. Lindbergh had written the book while vacationing in Captiva...The book's chapters reference a variety of shells Lindbergh used to symbolize the stages that women and relationships might experience. The sixth chapter is Argonauta and it begins:

'There are in the beach world certain rare creatures, the 'Argonauta' (Paper Nautilus), who are not fastened to their shell at all. It is actually a cradle for the young, held in the arms of the mother Argonaut who floats with it to the surface, where the eggs hatch and the young swim away. Then the mother Argonaut leaves her shell and starts another life.'

Rebecca felt this was a fitting description of her life at the time, as our boys were becoming less dependent and she gained a degree of independence as she prepared to re-enter the workforce."

ARION (43' RHODES WOODEN SLOOP) "Arion was a poet from Greek mythology whose ship was sunk and his gold stolen by bandits. He was tossed over the side but played his lute as a last request and a dolphin saved him."

ATALANTA (28' 1976 SABRE) "She is great for cruising solo or double-handed, slow upwind when racing, and built in Maine. The name was on the boat in 2004 when I bought her. Her homeport had been Gloucester. She succeeds ARABESQUE, which sank in May 2004, also a Sabre 28.

Atalanta has a significant place in ancient Greek lore, being the first militant feminist. She insisted on equality with the guys, whom she was able to outperform both as a runner and as a hunter. I am happy and proud to keep the name."

ATLANTIC WAVEDANCER (44' CAL) "My previous sailboat was a C&C 37 named 'Wave Dancer'. She was known by the long term cruising fraternity from New England through the Bahamas and the Caribbean. As it turned out, there were a number of other vessels in the US Coast Guard registry with that name. So that our current CAL 44 had a unique identity that friends at a distance (listening to SSB radio) would recognize, 'Atlantic Wavedancer' was chosen. The name also reflected our planned cruising domain.

There is also a dolphin pictured next to the name. The significance is that - - - when dolphins approached us in shoaling waters, they always came from the shallow water side of our boat to herd us to the deeper water. They have been our reliable 'sentinels of the sea'."

AT LAST (20' AQUASPORT) "At last we had a boat of our own!"

ATTITUDE (18' EASTERN) "Dinner talk when children were growing up."

AUBURN (25' CAPE DORY) "We named our boat Auburn because my husband, Roy, son, Alex and I are all redheads."

AUD'S POD (13' CHAMBERLAND DORY SKIFF) "My husband had this boat made for us and named it after me. We love Marblehead Harbor and we knew that rowing and sailing around this lovely harbor would bring us many pleasurable and memorable moments in our little boat. (Made in 1986 at The Landing School.)"

AUFBLITZEN (16.5 TOWN CLASS) "In 1955 my husband Jim and I had just returned from our six month dream tour of Europe by bicycle and motor scooter when a group of Marblehead friends persuaded us to get a Town Class sailboat, the largest and most active fleet in the harbor. We had loved Austria, Switzerland and Germany, so we got out the German dictionary. 'Das Blitz is a noun which means a 'lightning flash' and 'aufblitzen' is the verb 'to flash like lightning'. We liked the sound of it and it sounded fast! We've had a lot of fun over the years."

AVANTI (40' C&C) "Avanti in Italian means 'go forward'. AVANTI does that very nicely in light or strong wind. This is my second AVANTI and it too has given me much pleasure cruising the northeast from Maine to Long Island."

AVATAR (34' NORLIN) "From the Ralph Bakshi movie 'Wizards'. Avatar is the good wizard."

11

B ——

BALEEN (46' TRAWLER) "Name taken from a classic tugboat. A particular species of whale which is large and continuously feeding."

BALI HAI (26' C&C) "This name is taken from the movie 'South Pacific'."

BAND OF BROTHERS (13' BOSTON WHALER) "Owner has three sons."

BAND WAGON (38.8' 1983 BRISTOL) "This is our second Band Wagon; the first was a Pearson 35. A number of reasons the name works for us. 'Band Wagon' is one of the classic MGM Musicals staring Fred Astaire and Cyd Charisse about an aging musical hoofer attempting a comeback in a Broadway Show. As 'Singing in the Rain' is to movies, 'Band Wagon' is to theatre. We are all very dramatic!

I used to be in a Rock Band –a la 'Band' - We are a family of six creating somewhat of a circus atmosphere a la 'Wagon' - We had no choice but to jump on it!"

BANTRY (34' J105) "A 'Bantry' is a pulling boat, powered by oars. Lines taken from a French longboat captured by the Irish in the battle of Bantry Bay."

BARBAROSA (21' FISHING BOAT) "My boat was originally named Barbarosa for the odd red and copper spots I have in my beard (I have brown facial hair). However, my aunt recently informed me that the name of the ship that our ancestors came to America on from Russia was named the Barbarossa. So once verified, this would be quite the coincidence."

BEHIND BLUE EYES (21'THOMPSON) "Named after a song by the Who. The owners love the Who and also have blue eyes."

BELLEROPHON (27' HUNTER SLOOP) "I have been a sailor for the past 30 years and have had a couple of small sloops. For the last 20 years I have sailed our waters in a 27' Hunter Sloop named BELLEROPHON. So many boats have catchy or humorous names, many times with a play in words, but Bellerophon is a historical name of significance in two most interesting ways. In the days of fighting sail the Bellerophon (1782-1836), called Billy Ruffian as the jack tars of day could not well pronounce its name was a major ship of line in Lord Nelson's navy. It was highlighted in the famous Patrick O'Brien and C.S. Forester books as it was involved in the famous Napoleonic battles: the Glorious First of June, the Battle of the Nile, and Trafalgar. Napoleon surrendered to this mighty 74 gun ship in 1815, 6 weeks after Waterloo.

And that is where the second historical reference and the one of more pertinence to me arises. As a member of the Corinthian Yacht Club this past decade, the seal, emblem and race boat all carry the name of the winged horse of Corinth, Pegasus, with the motto 'prepared both to contend together as equals and to respond to any challenge'. It seemed most appropriate to name my boat Bellerophon as he was the greatest hero and slayer of monsters in Greek mythology and he did this all on his horse Pegasus. So the CYC has at least one other boat in its fleet that has significance to its standard bearer."

BETELGEUSE (28' SAN JUAN) "Betelgeuse is the name of a very bright star in the Orion constellation which I learned to find as a student. A variation of the spelling is also the name of a funny and bizarre movie which my kids liked, and was popular around the time we bought our boat."

BET-EM AGAIN (30' 210) "BET-EM represents the two sisters, Betsey and Emmy. Name started by my father, Hosmer A. Johnson, with his MB in the 30's. Then we named our 210 the same (#17-1946), then #144 BET-EM TOO, #157 & #279 BET-EM AGAIN."

BETSY JO (35' WOODEN FISHING BOAT) "Named for sister, Betsy and mother, Josephine. (This is a strip plank fishing boat built in 1960.)"

BETWEEN SEASONS (22' AQUASPORT) "Our family is a sports family. We play soccer in the fall, ski and skate in the winter, and play soccer in the spring. Between seasons, we boat, swim, tube, and fish in the summertime. Hence, the name of our boat."

BETWEEN THE SHEETS (44' F&C KETCH) "It's a good play on words. Boat prior to this was 'TWO SALTED NUTS'. Wherever we go, people remember us. We thought it up one day sitting 'between the sheets'."

BIANCA (42' Rand & THOMPSON) "This is a character in 'Taming of the Shrew'."

BIG BAD WOLF (38.3' BRISTOL – hull #1) "My first ocean boat, a Coronado 25, was named Big Bad Wolf. When I bought it, the season was well under way, so I decided to wait on changing the name. At the time, I was 25 and single. I received so much grief over the name that I decided to keep it. The name had originally been chosen by three little girls in the family from whom I bought the boat."

BILLYCLUB (28' SISU BASS) "The first boat we owned was a twenty-four foot Seaway Center Console. I am known as Billy. My son is known as Billy. Further, at the time of the purchase of the Seaway, I was Clerk of the First District Court of Essex and in that capacity I interacted with most of the Police Departments in Essex County. As you know, most police officers carry a billy club. Since my name is Billy, my son is a Billy and my boat was used basically as a clubhouse, we named it the Billyclub. I believe this is a double entendre relative to Billys' using the boat as our club, ie. Billyclub and that police men carry a billy club. We also had a tender named Black Jack."

BITTERSWEET (39' BRISTOL) "The boat has been named BITTERSWEET since its commissioning in '69. We purchased the boat in '93. We felt the name was appropriate. As you may know, boat ownership is 'bittersweet'."

BJ WEST (34' SEARAY) "Named after six grandchildren in their birth order: Brett, Jared, Wes, Emily, Sam and Tedd."

BLACK MAGIC (41' HINCKLEY) "When Black Magic joined the family, the owners recognized her potential to be responsible for special and unpredictable experiences which made this name for a beautiful-black sloop seem very appropriate."

BLACK MAGIC (30' BLACK WATCH) "Black Magic is a modified and redesigned Black Watch power boat with only the hull still recognizable as one of the Black Watches built by Ted Hood and designed by Ray Hunt. Black Magic is named after the owner's first boat, a black 110 that was raced in Marblehead from 1961 - 1965."

BLACK WATCH (35' HINCKLEY YAWL) "Our boat was originally named 'BLACK MARIGOLD'. Its second owner, a Scotsman, named her 'BLACK WATCH'. Black watch, a familiar tartan, is worn by the royal regimen that protects Edinburgh Castle. We liked the connotations of strength, safety and nobility of spirit; so kept the name when we bought her in 1986. By the way, her previous owner traded up, and named his new boat 'BLACK WATCH' too!"

BLUE SIDE UP (21' SEAWAY) "My husband was a pilot and it is a term they often used in aviation..... 'Keep the blue side up'. (Referring to the sky/ horizon) Our boat has a blue hull, and when I said to him that we always want to keep the blue side up, above the water, he said, 'Perfect!'"

BOADICEA (30' ETCHELLS) "Boadicea (original spelling: Boudicca) was the queen of the Ceni tribe in ancient Britain. When her husband Caractus died, she shocked everyone by taking over the leading, devastating raids against the Romans. When she was eventually defeated, she took poison rather than be captured. Her statue-riding a chariot is outside the Houses of Parliament."

BOB-CAT (32' CABIN CRUISER) "This name was taken from Bob(bie) and her daughter Cat(hy)."

BONNIE ELIZABETH (36' WOODEN FISHING BOAT) "Captained by my nephew, Jim …. Named for his daughter, Bonnie, and his mother and my sister, Elizabeth (Betsy)."

BOOMERANG (23' ROBALO) "As a function of how every key decision in our lives has come around to haunt us multiple times, we thought it appropriate to honor our choice of a power boat over sail with this name."

BOON'S FARM (22' Sea Pro) "We named the boat after our dog, Boondoggle, a lovable golden retriever, who loved the water and sadly passed away last summer."

BOUDICCA (35' J) "Boudicca was a British warrior queen who defended Britain against the Roman army in about 47 AD. (We are English and were looking for something war-like with British connotations!)."

BOUGIE (27' ISLAND PACKET) "Bougie, pronounced (BooJhe) is the French word for candle. It (BOUGIE) is a nickname for our daughter, Jennifer Olivia. Her initials are J.O.Y. and she is the light of our lives..."

BREAKING AWAY (23' SONAR) "Named after the movie."

BREEZIN (34' SABRE) "George Benson's Theme Song 'Breezin'."

BRISK III (19' RHODES 19) "Brisk = To reflect the 'brisk' winds that we look forward to sailing our boat in. Also, the speed we expected from our boat. III = To reflect the three owners."

BUCKEYE II (34' SABRE) "Moved to Marblehead as newlyweds from Ohio in 1956. Buckeye, a 210 class, raced with a large fleet & many friends. Buckeye II has cruised in Massachusetts, Maine, Rhode Island and the Bay of Fundy."

BUFFLEHEAD (30' MORGAN) "Our favorite duck. Resides in front of our house all winter."

BUNKY (23' SONAR) "Named after a dog that spent some time with a dog psychiatrist. When this boat owner and some friends were listening to funny stories about the dog's $250 per hour psychiatric sessions, they decided that this dog deserved a boat!"

C ——

CAIJEN (35' DUFFY & DUFFY LOBSTER BOAT) "This boat is named after the owner's two daughters, Caitlin and Jennifer."

CALYPSO (27'11" C&C 27MK III) "Sailboat named after Jacque Cousteau's world famous CALYPSO. Our family admired Cousteau's activities (protection of animals, conservation, etc…) and the association with his boat CALYPSO. Our children grew up sailing aboard our own CALYPSO in the Marblehead area.

Years later, in the Mediterranean Sea at Mallorca, my son was sailing with Ted Turner aboard the maxi boat CONDOR. One layover day Jacque Cousteau visited Ted Turner at the dock. Cousteau had his new boat there and they invited my son J.B., to go sailing with them aboard the new research vessel. Cousteau personally guided my son throughout the boat. This increased the importance of the name CALYPSO and its association with Jacque Cousteau."

CAMILLE (16.5' TOWN CLASS) "Her name is Camille. My wife and I have 2 wonderful boys, Oliver and Henry. If either of the boys was born a girl, her name would have been Camille. So our Townie sailboat Camille is the daughter we didn't have."

CANNONADE (38' LITTLE HARBOR) "When Bill and I bought our sailboat together in 1983, we wanted a name that reflected both our interests. Bill's previous boat was named ROARING BULL for the rocks off his home on Goldthwaite Beach; not appropriate for a NH woman I thought. Since both had had second homes in Franconia and our families skied Cannon Mountain, where we first met, the powerful name CANNONADE (meaning fusillade of cannon fire) seemed perfect for our lovely yacht."

CAPELLA (32' SAILBOAT) "Given the nature of sailing, we thought naming our boat with a celestial theme would be appropriate. Capella was our first choice, being the third brightest star in the northern sky. We did consider other names--Polaris and Evenstar were already taken. We liked Cassiopeia but couldn't figure out how to spell it. Capella was our first choice from the start and survived all challenges."

CASCO (35.5' BRISTOL) "She is named after CASCO Bay in Maine, where I spent my summers on an island."

CATCH 22 (30' ETCHELLS) "Since Etchells are racing boats and the logo is E22, the name Catch 22 is a play on the book/movie title and the fact that when you race, you are often trying to 'catch' a boat ahead of you."

CAVEAT (30' SHIELDS) "We bought it second-hand from a lawyer in Larchmont, NY and it had this name already painted on it. We have had too much inertia to effect a change. My partner...practices law, so the name is appropriate anyway. He had wanted to rename it DAWN TREADER after the boat in C.S. Lewis' Stories From Narnia."

20

CELAENO (32' AAGE NIELSEN DESIGNED LOBSTER BOAT) "Celaeno is a star in the constellation Pleiades. In Greek mythology, Atlas and the nymph Pleione had seven daughters – Alcyone, Merope, Celaeno, Taygeta, Maia, Electra, and Sterope. The daughters killed themselves and were turned into stars when Atlas turned into a mountain. (Or in another story, Jupiter turned them into doves and then stars to enable them to escape the attention of Orion.) Members of our family have been naming boats after the stars since at least the early 20's."

CELTIC LADY (16.5' TOWN CLASS) "With a name like O'Grady, my Irish heritage is a given and all things of beauty, grace and speed should have a female name, so it was a natural choice."

CHALLENGE (26' FORTIER LAUNCH) "Name from the Weld Ship Plaque, from the Weld Shipping line in the late 1800's."

CHANDELLE (22' CAL) "My father was a pilot during World War II. He taught the Free French how to fly. A 'chandelle' was the French term for a particularly graceful turn in an airplane. Dad thought it was the perfect description for a well executed tack as well. They sold the airplane and with the money, bought the boat. Hence, rolling over the money and reversing the direction by being on the water."

CHENANGO (32' SHARPS ISLAND EXPRESS) "I grew up on the Chenango River in upstate New York."

CHINOOK (41' 1967 HINCKLEY) "CHINOOK is the name of a very strong warm wind that blows down from the Canadian Rocky Mountains during the winter, melting away snow and raising spirits. Our family has strong ties with Canada, the mountains and all things wind."

CHOCK FULL OF NUTS (27' NAUSET) "With three sons and one daughter aboard with them, these owners felt that this name was appropriate! This is their third boat with this name."

CHOREVO (34' SAILBOAT) "Chorevo means 'I am dancing' (from choreography) in Greek. My husband and captain is Greek and we met in a dance class."

CHOUETTE (41' TARTAN) "Chouette, in French, along with being a barn owl, is also an adjective meaning something good/great, wow! We thought it appropriate. It is also a backgammon game with three or more players; a 'captain', 'man in the box' and 'advisors' – also appropriate."

CHRISTIAN MICHAEL (27' CHRIS CRAFT) "We originally owned an O'Day sailboat that we named Christian Michael after our first born child. As our family of three grew to a family of six, we moved from the world of sailing to power boating but kept the name the Christian Michael. We now have 4 children, and two grandchildren, so perhaps it's time we add a few more boats to the Marblehead Harbor."

CHRISTIE (39'10" CONCORDIA YAWL) "My wife's nickname was 'Christie' in college and we decided to use it on the boat."

CHUM II (30' RAMPAGE) "I am a partner in the boat with a good friend. We fish and use 'chum' to attract large fish. Therefore, friends fishing and owning a boat together = CHUM II."

CIRCE (30' SHIELDS) "By coincidence, I had decided to change the name of my boat to CIRCE just at the time I met my wife to be. She had a cat named Circe. I guess we both related to magic."

CITIUS (35.4' IOD) "Ex Puritan…Ex Stradivarius."

COMMOTION (30' FRERS) "It was very difficult. It had no name in Scituate. Then I mailed in ECLIPSOR and called the Coast Guard to change it to COMMOTION. Indicates motion, confusion, sometimes panic, but always creates a commotion."

COMPAS TRAVELER (17'6" AQUASPORT) "Named for Compass Travel Service, Inc., Atlantic Avenue, Marblehead..."

CONNOR B. (8' SKIFF) "Name for my late son, Raymond Connor Bates."

CORIOLIS (50' GULFSTAR KETCH) "Gaspard Gustave De Coriolis (1792-1843) studied dynamics of rotating machinery in France, and was lead to describing the deflections of ocean currents on the rotating earth. Known as the 'Coriolis Effect' of the 'Coriolis Force', it plays an essential role in oceanography and meteorology. All our sailboats over the years have been named CORIOLIS in his honor."

CORONA (30' S-2 9.1) "Too many beers one evening."

CORSAIR (30' PEARSON) "Newt Clemson called me about a Pearson 30' sailboat that had been repossessed that was up for sale. We visited the boat in a boatyard in Maine and decided to put in an offer. The boat's existing name was Looking Glass. We made an offer for the boat that was very much below the current market value and to our surprise it was accepted. Neither one of us liked the name Looking Glass as we thought it was too cutesy, cutesy. We decided that since we thought we had stolen the boat that it should have a name relating to pirates. The Barbary pirates had a small sailboat that they called a corsair. Thus, the name Corsair, which is a very fast small sailboat."

CRISTI III (31' CAPE DORY) "Combination of sons names, minus one letter each: Chris(topher), Tim(othy) = (CRISTI)."

CROCODILE (36' CARTER ONE TON) "Croc's dark green hull and pronounced IOR 'bumps' give her the appearance and character of a crocodile. Her name also appears to have been a reference to René Lacoste, nicknamed 'The Crocodile' for his aggressiveness on the tennis court."

CUKLA (24' 110) "Cukla is a Greek term of endearment; a phrase a father might use to address his young daughter."

CURRENT AFFAIRS (28' SABRE) "In 1984, I was single for the first time in twenty years. My new boat, a sport fisherman, was a change from my previous Pearson 30, and I knew someday I would be into sailing again. I needed a name that would suit both sail and power. I wanted a name I could use forever.

Current Affair – I was in the electrical wire harness and cable business (my electric Current Affair). Current Affair – I was involved with a beautiful woman who is now my wife (my Current Affair). Current Affair – We now own a Sabre 28 and are back to the affair of sailing and the importance of the ocean current."

CUTTAIL (21' EVERGLADE) "We started a fishing tournament with 2 other couples from Marblehead over 20 years ago, and the 'Cuttail Classic' brought many adults and kids to get on the water that may not have fished before.

Our friends, who moved to Vermont, had named their 1st boat Cuttail. We asked to continue the tradition and were granted permission to carry it on. A 'cuttail' is the nickname the apprentice fisherman was given for he would be the one to "cut" the corner of the tails of the caught fish, so the captain would know their count for the day."

CYCLONE (24' FOUR WINNS) "Lee and I met at Iowa State University, home of the 'Cyclones'. The CYCLONE name is from our Midwest roots!"

CYDONIA (44.5' MJM) "Cydonia is the Latin name for the quince, a fruit in the Rosaceae family, which also contains apples and pears. Our Falk family crest contains three golden quinces and my parents often made quince jam. Furthermore, Cydonia is an epithet of the Greek goddess Athena.

It is well-known that seven letters in the name of a vessel will ensure good luck, as will naming a boat after a goddess. Last, but not least, there is a connection to the stars: 1106 Cydonia is an asteroid in the main asteroid belt between Mars and Jupiter, and there is also a region of Mars called Cydonia, which borders the plains of Acidalia Planitia and the Arabia Terra highlands."

CYGNET II (45' CUSTOM AUX KETCH) "Been moored in the harbor since 1954. I used to own a company named White Swan. Big swan made little swan possible. Dinghy named THE EGG. (F.Y.I. A cygnet is a baby swan.) P.S. In 1916, mother thought up company name."

CYRENA (34' PALMER JOHNSON) "Named by a 'committee'. CYRENA was originally bought in partnership. The name was intended as an unusual variation of the Greek sirens. CYRENA is a sister ship of former British Prime Minister Edward Heath's first MORNING CLOUD."

HOME

AWAY FROM HOME

D ——

DAN CIN (25' CAPE DORY) "From Dan and Cindy; husband and wife owners..."

DANCING FEATHER II (32' SABRE) "We became fascinated with the original Dancing Feather which was a Boston Harbor pilot schooner operating in the outer harbor and beyond, in the mid 19th century. Pilot schooners had to be fast and quite seaworthy. This combination of features created a unique design that was a refinement for a hearty and speedy vessel. We see these sailing characteristics in our Sabre and like to think she is deserving of some of the admiration of her 19th century name sake."

DANISH D-LITE (30' PEARSON) "My girlfriend was a true Danish delight."

DARK & STORMY (22' MAKO) "So, being a fan of Bermuda for many reasons, including their famous drink, Dark & Stormy's, what could be better for a black hull boat?!!"

DARK HORSE (36' FRERS) "My wife, Rich and I spent months reviewing names and no one could agree. Then, on a trip to Tortola, B.V.I., we saw a boat named DARKHORSE and instantly decided we liked the sound of it. That was January '85 and the boat was christened in April '85."

DEGAGE (36' PEARSON) "Boat named Degage, a French word of English usage meaning nonchalant or casual. We race on another boat (called ACHIEVER) so the time spent on our cruising boat is deliberately low-key and relaxed; hence the name. One might say it means the opposite of 'racing' and all that goes with it."

DELIA (12.5' HERRESHOFF) "'Delia' is a love song sung by the Whiffenpoofs, with whom I sang at Yale 50 years ago: 'I wish I knew where Delia's gone, or why she went away, or if she always knew that she, would break my heart one day.' But my Delia today is always there, clinging happily to her mooring yet calling me, like a siren, to take her out to sea, to dance with her in the waves, the wind and the sunlight, and to bring her home."

DESCENTE (30' S-2 9.1) "...1. Act of falling or descending. 2. A downward inclination or slope. 3. A sudden incursion or attack. 4. A great name for a boat that a skier spends his summers sailing."

DESIRE (17' HOMEMADE LOBSTER BOAT) "Bennie Tutt built this boat in 1947 in his back yard. It is named after the boat that was manned by Marblehead seamen who escorted Washington on his famous journey across the Delaware River."

DEUCES WILD (37' HERITAGE ONE TON) "There are 5 - #2's in the sail number (22222)."

DISPATCH (42' HINCKLEY POWER) "Dispatch came from research into family ship names from the 18th and 19th century. The original Dispatch was from Boston but was also built in Maine and was even briefly registered in Marblehead. We decided that 'Dispatch' – as a noun or verb with the connotation of sending with speed to a destination – is an excellent choice for a powerboat."

DIVERSION (35' GOODY STEVENS) "Built E. Boothbay, 1958. Wooden sports fisherman. The name speaks for itself."

DOC'S HOLIDAY (33' CHRIS CRAFT) "My husband, Mike, is a physician and he truly feels like he's on a holiday when he's on the water. (And do you remember the character, Doc Holiday?)"

DOLCE VITA (23.5' POWER CRUISER) "In year 17 (of being on the mooring waiting list) we blindly purchased a well maintained newer boat that suited all our short list criteria... We named it Dolce Vita, Italian for sweet life.... and just 2 years later, after a life of 3 kids, life in the community, fixer-upper house experiences, job changes, and life's ups and downs.... we got our permanent mooring assignment... just 3 months before our 20th wedding anniversary."

DOUBLE FANTASY (25' IRWIN) "The name was on the boat when we purchased it. Double Fantasy is the name of a John Lennon album."

DOUBLE HEADER (30' BERTRAM) "Named because both owners grew up in Marblehead, have twins growing up in Marblehead, and it's a double engine power boat."

DOVE KEY (21' AQUASPORT) "A coastal bird who comes ashore only to mate."

DOWN BUCKET (13' WHALER) "'Trash' bucket and tender for racing sailboats."

DRAGONFLY (34' SABRE TARGA) "We are very fortunate to live on the water across from Browns Island, and every summer there is a week period when Dragonflies are all around our home and on the water. They are light, airy, quick, beautiful creatures that skim over the water effortlessly. We were looking to rename the Sabre we bought in Virginia last fall. While having dinner outside one evening and discussing new names, there they were all around us. A simple end to our discussion and this story.

 We believe she possesses all the Dragonfly qualities."

DRAGON LADY (38' LITTLE HARBOR) "The name goes back to many generations in the Grinnell family. My great grandmother lived in northern China and it was said that not only was she the most beautiful woman in all of the provinces, but that she possessed mystical charms. She was called the 'Dragon Princess'.

At this time, the Vikings in Norway were preparing to explore the western oceans. They sent a crew to capture this fabled princess who would perhaps enchant them on their long ocean voyage. After many months of trying to unravel the princess' alleged charms and meeting with failure, they set her adrift in a boat off Nantucket Island. They named this boat DRAGON LADY to warn all that this was no enchantress at all! The little DRAGON LADY drifted into the Saconnet River and landed in the Little Compton, Rhode Island, where she was rescued by a local fisherman who did find her enchanting and together they started the Grinnell clan in this country. Thus, our boat is named after my ancestor and my wife, both of whom have mystical powers."

DRAMBUOY (26' LYMAN CLASSIC) "Some 30 years ago, we purchased a 36' Chris Craft on Lake Winnipesaukee with the idea of spending the spring on it at the lake, and then trucking it to the coast for the trip to Marblehead. We stopped at a local pub to celebrate our purchase and to choose a name. After many 'drambuies', the bartender said that it appeared that the name was selected because that was all we were saying. Hence,

DRAMBUOY, and that name has been on seven boats in Marblehead."

DREAM MAKER (24' BENETEAU) "Ski trail on Bear Mountain at Killington, VT. A nice, fast, cruising trail with beautiful views on a sunny day. Our winter sport is skiing. Summer activity is sailing."

DUCKLING (9' HOOD OCEAN ONE-SAILING DINGHY) "It looks like a little, fat duckling sitting in the water."

DULCINEA (36' OHLSON) "In 'Man of LaMancha', the near-sighted Don Quixote falls madly in love with a bar girl of doubtful reputation. He is unable to see any of the lady's flaws which are so apparent to everyone else. His love completes his mind's image of the perfect beauty of his Dulcinea.

Although I have no experience with such ladies, I do think this sort of myopia is an appropriate gift for living with a wooden boat."

DUTCHESS REGAL (16'6" DUCHESS REGAL) "Note the make and model. We are very innovative."

DYAYNU (18.5' CAPE DORY) "'Dyaynu' has been our Cape Dory Typhoon's name for nearly 45 years! We decided on that Hebrew word because it means 'Whatever God gives us is enough', or 'It's sufficient'... For three generations, our family has proudly sailed the Dyaynu in and out of Marblehead Harbor, mostly in. For us, that's usually enough!"

E ——

EL DORADO (14' LASER) "El Dorado is a metaphor representing something special and, unattainable. Anyone who races Lasers understands this! El Dorado is always just around the corner."

ELEVATION (23' EASTERN) "Being our first boat as a wedded couple, my husband and I wanted our boat's name to reflect the beginning of our married life together. When we were planning our honeymoon, we scheduled it so that we would be able to attend the U2 concert at Slane Castle in Ireland. The U2 tour was named Elevation."

ELIZABETH M (42' MARINER COMMERCIAL HULL) "ELIZABETH M is named after my wife of 54 years. She is actually the 3rd ELIZABETH M we have owned and we have had this one for 33 years. Boats have always been part of our family. All four of our boys grew up on boats. ELIZABETH M is considered to be one of the first 'Lobster Yachts' ever produced."

E~LOTUS (17' AQUASPORT) "The name originated from the Lotus cars (of which we have owned 6), every Lotus model name begins with an E (Elise (our latest Lotus), Elan, Elite, Eclat, Esprit, etc. The cars are built in England. The founder of the company was Anthony Bruce Colin Chapman (who was murdered by John Delorean)."

EMMA ROSE (36' CAL) "My daughter's name."

EMME G (26' FORTIER) "The name of our boat comes from the first name of our daughter and her and her mother's middle initial."

EMOTIONAL RESCUE (24.5' WALK AROUND CABIN CRUISER) "She's a 24.5ft walk around cabin cruiser my family and I have owned for over 12yrs. Her name is the result of driving home from J&W Marine and having her namesake come on my radio by the Rolling Stones. And then to think about how perfect an irony given being on the water is such an emotional rescue across many layers of professional and personal moments in life."

ENDEAVOUR (26' SISU) "There were several reasons we settled on our boat's name, one of which is the affiliation with the quote 'Endeavour to Persevere'. Seems to be fitting for us since to endeavour is to strive for something. We waited many years for both the boat and the mooring, and now are delighted to have both!"

ENDORFIN (24' CENTER CONSOLE FISHING BOAT) "We came up with the name 'EndorFin' as a play on words of endorphin, because I am an avid fisherman and my wife is a nurse practitioner. We figured the name was well suited."

ENTERPRISE (27'6" HERRESCHOFF) "The boat is 75 years old. I have been restoring her and sailing her for 7 years. She is at once, old and new. A link to the past and future. As such, she embodies all that is nonperishable; strength, beauty, courage, heart, and the need to explore. She is a starship."

EPIC (40' FARR) "Originally built in New Zealand and named EPIC LASS. Raced in the 1985 Admiral's Cup and forced to change the name to EPIC because of conflict with sponsor Epic Glass. Bought and moved to Chicago in 1987 by previous owner who then moved to Conn. and campaigned on Long Island. Purchased by Eliot…after boat was donated to the Naval Academy in 1993."

ESADA (27'8" HUNTER) "ESADA stands for 'Eat S___ And Die Ass____', which is what sailors say to each other at the beginning of a race in Antigua each year."

ESCAPADE (30' INTERNATIONAL 210) "My wife decided that each 'trip' in the 210 WAS an escapade. Hence, the name."

ESCAPE (20' SEARAY) "We needed an escape!"

ES-CAP-E (31' PEARSON) "In the movie, 'Finding Nemo', Dory is trapped and sees a sign on a door. She reads it aloud, 'Es-cap-e' and then says, 'I wonder what that means? That's funny. It's spelled just like the word, escape.'"

ESTRELLITA (22'8.5" LIPPINCOTT-STAR CLASS) "This was the original name of the boat in the Star Class log. We all know it is bad luck to change the name of a boat."

EUGENE T. CONNOLLY (20' POWER) "This boat was named after a good friend and long time mentor."

EVANGELINE (21' FREEDOM) "In my family, every man previous to my grandfather, had been a schooner fisherman; first out of Tusket, Nova Scotia and later, Gloucester. This meant that the last of the seafaring women of the family was my great grandmother, Evangeline Doucette. My boat was named in the honor of her."

EXTRA INNINGS (BOSTON WHALER) "We eventually bought this boat for fishing and when the winds are not good for sailing. This is named 'Extra Innings' because it gives us extra time on the water when we cannot sail."

EYORE (30' ETCHELLS) "This boat was purchased during a time that the owner was taking care of a friend's car with the CT license plate EYORE. Unfortunately, during the car's stay in Marblehead, the boat owner's son managed to damage the car by 'T-boning' the car of a Pleon Yacht Club neighbor. After looking at the EYORE license plate for three months and discussing the 'EYORE accident' several times, the owner thought that EYORE would be a good name for his boat."

F ———

FAIR SUSAN (32' SABRE) "This is our third boat since 1976 with this name. We don't recall its origin, but I'm sure we had a good reason. We still think it's a good name. It must have been from fair winds and Susan (Susan is the name of one of the owners)."

FAIRWIND (32' C&C) "Being a sailboat, what more could any sailor wish for but fair winds and following seas. Hence the name, FAIRWIND."

FALL***LINE (22' MAKO) "When we moved from racing our Rhodes 19 to a classic Mako power boat, I wanted a name that reflected our love of skiing and my involvement with the sport as a ski instructor. The Fall Line is the fastest most direct route down a mountain. The Fall line is often referred to in teaching a parallel turn as in, 'across the Fall Line', or 'down the Fall Line'.

It complimented the transition from sailing to power on the water..."

FANDANGO (21' QUICKSTEP) "When the Argonauts got to the top of the highest pass in the Sierras, they danced the Fandango to celebrate that event. Celebrations are good... agree?"

FANDANGO (50' 1967 COLUMBIA SLOOP) "We first heard of the boat name Fandango many years ago when we saw an ad for an 85' classic wood ketch in an old boating magazine. It was an unusual and intriguing name that we haven't often seen on boats, and it just stuck with us. So when we acquired our boat in 2000, the name was already in our heads. Fandango is a style of lively Spanish music and dance - we love to dance but have never tried it - and the name kept rising to the top of our short list. It seemed a good fit to name our 13' Whaler 'Tango'. By the way, the word 'fandango' can also mean light hearted, whimsical, foolish, and we all know we have to be a little bit of that to own a boat!"

FANTASEA (33' PEARSON) "Previous name was GYPSEA. Buying a 33' sailboat was a dream we didn't expect to be fulfilled for many years. We were surprised it happened as fast as it did. Thus, it was a fantasy that came true."

FARAWAY (43' CUSTOM S&S YAWL) "My grandparents wintered in Chicago, Illinois and summered in Maine. In that era, many houses were given names that were part of the address. The house name was 'FARAWAY' due to its great distance from Illinois. Thus, our boat is named after a house."

FAR NIENTE (22' WEBBERS COVE) "Shopping for a powerboat, I loved the classic, Downeast picnic style Webbers Cove boat I found. Beautiful, black hull, gorgeous lines, appeared to be in good shape. Perfect. I was shopping for a boat with a friend and boat partner who is also a fan of all things Italian (We were recently back from a big trip to Sicily, in fact). Our ambitions for the boat were modest: local cruising, and of course a platform for hanging out with some adult beverages. Then I saw the name of the boat: 'Far Niente'. It means 'doing nothing'. Perfect. :)"

FAT CAT (22' AQUASPORT) "FAT CAT is our initials. We also believe it is the oldest Aquasport in Marblehead Harbor."

FE (20' AQUASPORT) "The name came from the periodic table of elements. It is the chemical symbol of iron and in relation to my last name."

FEARLESS (26' FORTIER LAUNCH) "Name from the Weld Ship Plaque from the Weld Shipping Line in the late 1800's."

FENWICK (21' WOODEN CATBOAT) "Fenwick C. Williams, of Marblehead, designed this 21' Catboat and was a great friend of mine. Therefore, the name had to be 'FENWICK'."

FIDDLEHEAD (25' HUNT) "We purchased our boat and loved the name it came with - Bluegrass (the hull is blue). The seller from CT, however, requested that we change it, and we didn't want to acquire any bad boat name mojo by not complying! We wanted to relate the new name to the old, and started to think of bluegrass instruments. So we named her Fiddlehead (this is also a common carving on the prow of old wooden ships, as well as a harbinger of warm weather in New England gardens!)."

FIDELITY (29'10" PEARSON COASTER) "I worked for Fidelity and received a good bonus."

FIFTEEN TWO (32' CW HOOD) "The name refers to a term in the card game of Cribbage. Sharon and I try to play often, especially on the boat. My father, Captain 'Bunny' Russell, loved the game. I have many memories playing with him and feel he would approve of the name."

FINALLY (21' PURSUIT) "We gave the name FINALLY to our boat in 2004. The lettering is in the Red Sox font."

FIN & TONIC (41' ALBEMARLE SPORTFISH EXPRESS) "We have been visiting the Abacos for decades, Elbow Key specifically, and there used to be a simple fishing club and thatched roof bar called the Fin & Tonic Club. We liked the idea for our 1st boat name and it has stuck ever since. It fits."

FINGER PRINTS (30' GRAMPIAN) "The kids went to work on it when it was new. Dad thought of the name as it was the first thing that came to his mind."

FINN McCOOL (30' PEARSON) "From the Irish story, The Legend of Knockmany. Finn McCool was a mythical Irish giant who was being pursued by the evil Cucullen. Finn's wife, Mrs. McCool, was the brave and ingenious heroine in the story, who plotted and carried out the tactic to be rid of Cucullen."

FINS UP (41' ALBEMARLE SPORTFISH EXPRESS) "3 sons and a Buffett fan father."

FIREWOOD (36' 1957 BEAL'S ISLAND LOBSTERBOAT) "When purchased off of a survey 'sight-unseen' in 1995, this 1957 Beal's Island Lobsterboat was not a pretty sight. Upon boarding the boat for the first time, a partner in the boat exclaimed, 'It's just FIREWOOD.' Two years later, the beautiful boat you see now emerged from the shed in better-than-new condition."

FISHIN' MAGICIAN (20' AQUASPORT) "Named because Mike was a head basketball coach at MHS – team name, Magicians. Also, he is an active sport and commercial rod & reel fisherman."

FITSEA (35.5' BRISTOL) "Our last name is Fitzpatrick and my husband's friends have always called him 'Fitz' or 'Fitzy'. When thinking of names for the boat, our son, who was about 7 at the time, said, 'How about Fitzy?' We changed the spelling to a more boat worthy name. It's unique and to our knowledge there is no other boat with that name."

FIVE SEAS (30' PURSUIT OFFSHORE) "At the time we named our boat, there were five members of our family with the last name beginning with a C, and we (my wife and I) had travelled on five of the seven seas."

FLIP (17' BOSTON WHALER) "The boat flipped over in 38 degree water in Salem Harbor. It used to be called Grunt."

FLOWER POT (19' RHODES 19) "The Flower Pot is a famous Pub in Aston - Henley on Thames, England that we were lucky enough to live next door to. We rented our house from the Publican who ran it whilst we lived in the UK for 5 years."

FLY BY (24' LIMESTONE) "Fly By was the caretaker's horse who lived on Naushon Island and we'd see him most summers walking the beach in Tarpaulin Cove when I was a little kid."

FLYING COLORS (21' POWERBOAT) "She is named Flying Colors in honor of our flag as well as because she flies effortlessly and beautifully over the waves."

FLYING ELVIS (31' SPORT TENDER) "My wife came up with the name knowing that the Patriots logo was inspired by Elvis, and Bob Kraft calls the logo the Flying Elvis."

FLYING FISH (28' 1983 BERTRAM) "The Flying Fish name first gained notoriety in Marblehead from the fast schooner of that name which sailed captained and crewed out of Marblehead with the captain's wife, as a navigator, which was very unusual for that time. The first three versions of Marine Aviation Burgess Planes built in Marblehead were also named the 'Flying Fish'.

The Flying Fish was designed by Jeremiah Burnham, the famous shipbuilder, and was launched in Essex, Massachusetts, in 1860. For more than 20 years the Flying Fish was the most representative ship of the market schooner class and was taken as a model by shipbuilders of the time. Because of its unusual construction features and huge sail area, the Flying Fish was one of the fastest schooners in the Gloucester fishing fleet and these unique characteristics made it capable of carrying the catch of fish from the famous Grand Banks to the ports where it was sold with the obvious advantages of reaching the market first."

FOGDOG (30'CROSBY HAWK) "It's a bright spot or beam of light sometimes seen in a fog bank when the sun starts to burn thru. We named previous boats after our dogs. We liked this weather term [from the fact that it accompanies fog as a dog accompanies its owner]-dictionary explanation. Also parallels an experience the owner of the boat had as a youngster. Being lost in the fog for 3 days!"

FOGGY NOTION (17' PRINCE CRAFT) "Being an avid cod fisherman, I often travel 5-10 miles offshore to reach my favorite fishing spots. I navigate by means of a compass and triangulate from visual sightings. On days when the fog is too dense to locate my visual sightings, I will simply take a compass heading and travel offshore until 'it feels right'.

Since I seemed to have better luck in 1986, (the year I named the boat) on foggy days when I was only guessing my exact location due to my lack of instruments; I thought FOGGY NOTION was a good phrase that captured the nature of my luck as a cod fisherman. I also was a fan of Lou Reed & the Velvet Underground, which have a song by that title."

FOO (23' SEACRAFT) "She was named after the Star boat FOO, that my grandfather developed rod rigging on."

FOOTNOTE (8.5' INFLATABLE) "This boat is the tow along dinghy for HISTORIAN'S CRAFT. One of the owners teaches a course in historical methodology, historiography, research, and writing, that is called Historian's Craft."

FOUR BUOYS (23' REGULATOR) "Our family has four boys, so we thought an appropriate name for our boat would be Four Buoys."

FRAID KNOT (20' GRADY WHITE) "Have you heard the joke about the string that walked into the bar? 'Fraid knot' is the punch line!"

FREETIME (19' SEA RAY) "Obviously, we never have enough time in our life to relax. So when we're on our boat, it's our free time."

FRENCH CURVES (22' CATALINA) "I wanted a name that would have more than one meaning. Something that could be a bit sassy. I also wanted something that would reflect something personalized. I'm a graphic artist and French curves are plastic templates that are used to draw smooth curves."

FRESH START (23' SONAR) "The boat was purchased just after retiring, hence, a fresh start."

FULL CIRCLE (33' CAPE DORY) "I grew up in Marblehead and after college, worked in St. Thomas, then moved back to Marblehead and then to Denver, Colorado. My wife Cathy grew up in Belfast, Maine. She then lived in Portland, Maine, Boston, Denver, Wellington, New Zealand and Denver again.

We met in Denver and both decided we had been away from the ocean and our families long enough so we moved back to Marblehead. We decided our lives had come 'Full Circle'."

FUTOMAKI (34.5' CATALINA) "Futomaki means 'veggie-roll' in Japan. It's a form of sushi, which is rice and raw fish. We always feel so relaxed on our boat and often joke that we feel like 'veggies' out on the ocean sailing around."

HOCUS POCUS

Great American IV

G ——

GADGET (19.5' CORINTHIAN) "Years ago, I built a Lightning Class sailboat and it had so many fittings, ropes, and controls; I decided to call it GADGET."

GAIL FORCE (20'9" STINGRAY) "For years, I have been living with a tempest named Gail. This pint size hurricane has the fury of a full blown two flagger and I thought it only appropriate to name my boat after this gale on two legs.

P.S. The boat has been places and seen weather you wouldn't believe! A past sailor, or ragman, wouldn't lie!"

GEMINI (26' PACESHIP) "I supply sailcloth tape to sail makers. One of the styles of rope with tape that was very popular was called Gemini, for its twin rows of stitched rope. I may have sold enough tapes over the past 15 years to pay for the purchase of my GEMINI."

GEMINI (23' SEA SPRITE) "Twin boys!"

GENERAL JOHN GLOVER (26' U.S. COAST GUARD SURF BOAT) "This is the boat Glover's Regiment has used since 1979 to celebrate Marblehead's key role in the Christmas night victory at Trenton in 1776. It is the town's official Colonial Welcoming boat."

GIN RICKY (13.8' SUNFISH) "Alcoholic drink, but names of owners are Gin and Ricky."

GIRLS, GIRLS, GIRLS (18' GRADY WHITE) "Three girls in the family."

GITANA (61' MOTOR VESSEL) "E.Y.C. flagship 1887-1888. 115' (LOA) schooner owned by Commodore William F. Weld; great uncle to Charlie... (It means 'gypsy' in Spanish)"

GLOBAL HOPE II (19' HOMEMADE) "Named after the tanker that went aground on Cunny Ledge, outside Salem Harbor during the 'Blizzard of 1978'. Named by the owner of the boat shop that did the wiring and motor for the boat."

GOLDEN COD (23' RUNABOUT) "This boat is named after the owner's Bed and Breakfast, 'The Golden Cod'. The boat is used for fun fishing and harbor excursions."

GOLDENEYE (37' JEANNEAU) "Quack! It's a duck. I'm Captain Duck, Chief Duck of..."

GONZO (28' ALBIN TOURNAMENT EXPRESS) "Symbolizes the reckless and honest sincerity missing in the world of mass media and politics in general."Gonzo" journalism is a style of journalism that is written without claims of objectivity, often including the reporter as part of the story via a first-person narrative. The word "gonzo" is believed to be first used in 1970 to describe an article by Hunter S. Thompson, who later popularized the style. It is an energetic first-person participatory writing style in which the author is a protagonist, and it draws its power from a combination of both social critique and self-satire. It has since been applied to other subjective artistic endeavors."

GOOD JUDGEMENT (35' NIAGRA) "For 30 years we always asked our children (6) to use good judgment in their activities, trips, evenings and relationships. Now it's time for us to use good judgment."

GOOD QUESTION (30' CATALINA) "'What's the name of your new boat?' – 'Hmm, good question. Don't know yet. Still thinking.'
'Why did you buy that boat?' – 'Hmm, a bunch of reasons, good question.'
'What's the name of your boat?' 'Good Question.'"

GOTSCH'A (20.5' BOSTON WHALER OUTRAGE) "I'm known as 'Gotsch' by close friends and associates. Our 2 homes in Marblehead of over 45 years were known as 'Gotschport' and our Sugarloaf condo is 'Gotschaus'. Therefore, all of our important acquisitions had our last name involved. It's been and still is fun to use our tag line... Our Seattle son and family call their house, 'GotschportWest!'"

GRAVITATION (6' WOODEN DINGHY) "This is the dinghy for a Town Class called LEVITATION."

GREAT AMERICAN IV (60' IMOCA OPEN) "In 1989, the 60' trimaran **Great American** was sailed from New York to San Francisco by way of Cape Horn by George Kolesnikovs and Steve Pettengill. They beat the clipper Flying Cloud's record of 89 days arriving in 77 days.

Having an idea to engage K12 students by connecting them to a live ocean adventure, overflowing with science, geography and math, I acquired the boat in spring 1990 for an attempt on the record from San Francisco to Boston by way of Cape Horn set by the clipper Northern Light in 1853. I invited Steve Pettengill to sail with me. We kept the name **Great American** because we felt it was appropriate for the route, between two great American ports, had the grandeur of many of the great clipper names, and would be appreciated by American schoolchildren.

With 400 schools following our Ocean Challenge Live! K12 program weekly by newsletter, Steve and I raced against the clipper Northern Light's time (we had an abstract of her logbook). 400 miles west of Cape Horn, we were capsized in a horrific storm with 85 knots of wind and seas officially estimated at 65' (National Weather Service). 90 minutes later, we were re-righted by a wave, the first time in history that a capsized trimaran at sea had been righted by a wave. 17 hours later, we were rescued by New Zealand Pacific (who had 20 meter seas recorded in her logbook), an 815' refrigerated containership. We were 18 days to Holland with them.

Ultimately, **Great American**, dismasted and swamped, rounded Cape Horn and continued eastward, finally fetching up on the west coast of South Georgia Island, about 20 miles south of where Ernest Shackleton had landed. We never went to look; we thought that she was in good spiritual company there.

In 1993, we acquired a 50' French trimaran - Dupon Duran II – and re-named her **Great American II** in honor of that first great boat whose massive strength had kept her from breaking up off the Horn. With GA2, we sailed 1993 San Francisco-Boston (California Gold Rush), 2001 New York-Melbourne (Australian Gold Rush), and 2003 Hong Kong- New York (China Tea Trade) record passages, plus the singlehanded Transat 2004 (UK-USA). Each of those Ocean Challenge Live! school programs reached over 200,000 students. She was sold in 2004.

In 2006 we acquired a French Open 60, Solidaires, built by Thierry Dubois, for the 2008 Vendee Globe, solo, non-stop, around-the-world. We re-named her **Great American III**, and ultimately finished 9th of 11 finishers of 30 starters in 121 days over 28,790 non-stop miles, and most importantly, reaching about 250,000 student participants. She was sold in 2010 to Derek Hatfield of Canada for another round-the-world race.

In 2013, we acquired a Swiss Open 60, Mirabaud, from Dominique Wavre, for Vendee Globe 2016. We re-named her **Great American IV**. She sits proudly at the mouth of Marblehead Harbor as we prepare for the November 2016 start in Les Sables d'Olonne, France."

GREEN MACHINE (30' ETCHELLS) "Dartmouth football team. Boston Celtics."

GREYHOUND (22.5' BANKS COVE) "Its name was the name of a ship that belonged to the W.F. Weld & Company shipping fleet. W.F. Weld was owned by ancestors of Jay's family."

GUARDIAN DUCK (40' MD-40) "This boat was built over a 10 year period, next to Redd's Pond in Marblehead. Redd's Pond is frequently called 'The Duck Pond'. GUARDIAN DUCK has looked down on several generations of Marblehead ducks."

GULLWING (30' CW HOOD WASQUE) "The name is a nickname for a 1950's Mercedes Benz 300 SL Coupe that has doors that open upward, and resemble a gulls wings. My occupation is restoring, and buying / selling theses cars."

GURNET (43' OCEAN ALEXANDER) "My wife's grandfather always named his boats 'GURNET', after the lighthouse off of Duxbury."

GWENDOLEN (22' SISU LOBSTER STYLE) "My boat was named after my sister who passed away in 1993, at the age of 36, to breast cancer."

GYPSY (25' BHM COMMERCIAL LOBSTER BOAT) "Name came when the boat was purchased in 1989."

GYPSY (33' IOD) "This wooden boat was built in Norway. Since it seems to have been passed around frequently and has never really had a permanent home, the name GYPSY seemed fitting."

H ——

HAFA ADAI (35.25' J109) "Hafa Adai is named in Honor of Celeste's father, Juan Ignacio. He grew up on the South Pacific Island of Guam where he joined the US Navy during WWII. Mr. Ignacio served aboard the USN Ramapo in the Pacific and was a Pearl Harbor survivor, his ship being spared though in port at that time. Hafa Adai (pronounced as one word 'half-a-day') simply means 'Hello' in the Chamorro language of Guam, the western most American territory."

HANNAH GLOVER (63' U.S.C.G. 149 PASSENGER LUNCH AND DINNER BOAT) "Peter and I were in the National Grand Bank completing some boat paperwork, when we quickly needed a boat name to fill in. I ran into Bette Hunt, a Historical Society member and friend, and asked her quickly for a boat name of a famous Marblehead girl or woman. She first said 'Susannah Glover', daughter of General Glover. I thought that was too long. She then suggested 'Hannah Glover', wife of General Glover, and the rest is history!"

HAPPINESS IS (22' AQUASPORT) "We bought the boat new, back in 1968 and 'happiness is', was a common saying at that time.

To us, 'happiness is' being out on the waters off Marblehead. We were the first Aquasport in Marblehead Harbor!"

HAPPY (18' HOMEMADE) "Built in 1944. This boat was built by John Hartred (airline pilot) of Gallison Avenue, Marblehead. Sold to Laurie Bell of Gregory Street, Marblehead, who named her HAPPY. I purchased it in 1955 and have retained ownership ever since."

HARBINGER II (34' CATALINA) "Harbinger II is the second sailboat to have been given the Harbinger name. The first sailboat was given that name because we felt it was the harbinger of better things and times. As the robin is the harbinger of spring we liked the message it carried. When Harbinger was replaced with the current sailboat, carrying on the Harbinger theme was appropriate."

HARBOR COURT (28' BERTRAM F.B. CRUISER) "We live on a small, private street called 'Harbor Court'."

HARD TACK (32.9' BRISTOL) "I have found from my sailing experience that when tacking upwind, there is usually one tack that is rougher and less comfortable than the opposite tack. That to me is a hard tack. In old sailing days, that is until the 20th century, a staple on board any sea going boat, military or civilian, was a bread, more like a biscuit, that is known as hard tack. Hard Tack is named with both of those things in mind. This Bristol sloop rigged, sailboat was designed and built in Marblehead by Ted Hood."

HAT TRICK (16' BOSTON WHALER) "When the boat was first purchased, the two owners and a niece were on it constantly. Since there were three people always on the boat, and one of the owners was a Marblehead hockey enthusiast; the name HAT TRICK seemed perfect!"

HAVOC (30' OLSON) "Look and see!"

HEADERNAUT (26' MACGREGOR) "Someone from Marblehead is a 'header'. A header is also a sailing term for when the wind shifts onto your nose. 'Naut' means voyager (originally, sailor). It's also, of course, a homophone for 'knot' and 'not'. We liked the word play."

HEART'S DESIRE (35.5' BRISTOL) "When we bought the boat we felt it was just the perfect sailboat for family cruising and we passed papers on Valentine's Day. We have thoroughly enjoyed it."

HEART THROB (34' PEARSON) "A heart throb is your first passionate love. As a cardiologist, this seemed especially appropriate for the boat and sport we fell in love with."

HEELTAPPER (38' CONTROVERSY) "A long time ago, Marbleheaders were called Heeltappers. It resulted from a bad storm wiping out many of the fishing boats from Marblehead. The Marbleheaders resorted to the cottage industry of making shoes. When one would walk by their houses, there would be a tap-tap-tap sound. Hence, they became known as Heeltappers."

HERITAGE (63' 12 METER) "Original name at launch date of 1970."

HIATUS (26' COLUMBIA) "This 26' sloop was purchased by Richard Robbins and Leonard...in 1970. It is a 1969 fiberglass boat. Robbins and Leonard were partners in an ad agency. Hiatus is the time when ads are not running, a respite, the time between. Sandra...and Leonard...have been partners for many years."

HIGH C's (36' SABRE SPIRIT SLOOP) "The name comes from our love for opera and is an homage to the great Luciano Pavarotti, who as a young man, was known as 'King of the High C's'.

The boat name is written on a musical staff and the letter 'g' in 'High' is a 'G Clef'. The apostrophe between the 'C' and 's' is a high C."

HIGH FLIGHT (19.5' CORINTHIAN SLOOP) "I purchased my boat in 1966 and it is the only boat I've ever owned. We've been through a lot together, and both of us are a little worse for the wear, but I still love her. She is named after the poem 'High Flight' by John Gillespie Magee, Jr.. It brought together many of the wonders of aviation that I have experienced since age 12 as an aircraft spotter, a teenage Civil Air Patrol cadet and later a Navy fighter pilot. As a boat, this one is beautiful and wonderful, and it just goes with the thoughts in the poem."

HIGHWAY 17 (24' SEAFOX) "Highway 17 is the highway from San Jose, CA. to Santa Cruz, CA. Growing up, we traveled that road weekly to get to our beach house and the ocean!"

HIPER STRIPER (26' BOSTON WHALER) "Named after an inside family joke."

HISTORIAN'S CRAFT (26' PEARSON) "One of the boat owners is an historian and professor of history. She also teaches a course in historical methodology, historiography, research and writing required of undergraduate majors – a course she created called Historian's Craft. Our tow along dinghy is FOOTNOTE."

HOLGER DANSKE (42'6" CUSTOM) "When my husband and I had HOLGER DANSKE built in Denmark in 1964, we wanted a Danish name for her and did quite a lot of research in libraries over there. We learned about Holger Danske (literally, 'Holger, the Dane'), a semi-mythical Danish hero from the time of Charlemagne. There is a large statue of Holger in the dungeon at Kronborg Castle (Hamlet's castle) in Elsinore, Denmark.

Holger is asleep and the Danish belief is that he will awaken when Denmark is in trouble and save the country. So it seemed to us a good and meaningful name for our boat. As far as we could learn, only one other boat had ever been named HOLGER DANSKE and that was a famous Danish ice breaker."

HOME RUN (36' C&C) "We bought our first real boat in the spring of 2000. It was a C&C 29 sailboat. In 2007 we upgraded to a C&C 36 and kept the same name. Our two boys were 4 and 7 in 2000 and they both loved baseball. I love double entendres. We had a family naming contest and came up with the name Home Run. It became our summer 'Home' and went downwind on a 'run' on our trips to Down East Maine."

HOPEWELL (38' EASTBAY) "This spring, when trying to figure out a name for our new boat, friends were solicited for ideas. Pam Cassidy did some research on our last name of Whitmore, which historically dates back to 1066 in England, and discovered that Whitmore ancestors came to America in 1635 aboard a vessel named HOPEWELL. Through subsequent research, we discovered the other side of my father's family, Benson, had also emigrated to America aboard the same vessel a year earlier in 1634. Thus the name."

HOSANA (18' BRITISH ALACRITY) "Original name. Purchased used."

HOT SPUR (36' FRERS) "Girl at work."

HOWL (35' BALTIC) "I (used to) go out and HOWL. She (my wife) says, 'How will he pay for it?'"

HURRAH (49' EASTBAY) "When I got divorced a friend said, 'This could be your last hurrah.' I said, 'Not my last but what a grata name for my new boat.' Hence 'Hurrah'."

HURRICANE (22' AQUASPORT) "The name is derived from the fact that the boat is speedy."

HURRICANE (23' PARKER) "I am probably the only person who has had TWO boats sunk at their mooring in Marblehead harbor due to storms, neither of which was 'supposed' to be that bad. The first, was a Peterson 42 racing sailboat named 'Fat Tuesday' which broke off the mooring, along with about five other boats at the mouth of the harbor, and was beaten to death on Gerry Island due to an October nor'easter in 1988.

The second boat was my Sisu 22 bass boat named 'Tango' which filled with water and sank at its mooring when Hurricane Jeanne brushed by New England in 2004. Again, the size of the waves in the harbor far exceeded any forecast. After the insurance company totaled that boat, I took the money and bought my Parker. I named it 'Hurricane', hoping that honoring the storm would keep the boat safe. So far, so good!"

HUSKY (30' NONSUCH) "The owners took one look at the stern of this boat and determined that it looked like a 'pretty husky beast'. A Husky is the name of a Canadian animal. As the owners are originally from Canada, they liked the double meaning."

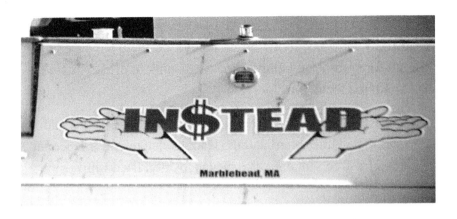

Marblehead, MA

I——

IMUS McHUGH (30' GRADY WHITE) "As my husband said, when he saw the 30' Grady for the first time, 'He is a 'big boy'.' So, we decided to dedicate this 'big boy' to our recently departed 130 lb. 'big boy' -- a black labrador/malamute mix rescue dog named Imus."

INDRA (34' S-2) "It's the goddess of the ocean."

INISFAIL (34' MJM POWER) "The boat's name comes from a mythical Irish place as described in <u>The Book of Leinster</u> in the 14th century (below): 'The Wooing of Etain'

'Fair Lady, will you come with me to wondrous land where there is music? Hair is like the blooming primrose there; smooth bodies arc the color of snow. There is neither mine nor yours; bright are teeth, dark are brows. A delight to the eye, blackbird's eggs; though fair to the eye, Mag Fail, it is a desert next to Mag Mar. Intoxicating, the ale of this Inisfail; more intoxicating by far that of Tir Mar. A wonderful land that I describe: youth does not precede age. Warm sweet streams throughout the land, your choice of mead and wine. A distinguished people without blemish, conceived without sin or crime. We see everyone everywhere, and no one sees us: the darkness of Adam's sin prevents our being discerned. Woman, if you come to my bright people, you will have a crown of gold for your head; honey, wine, fresh milk to drink you will have with me there, Fair Lady.'"

INISFREE (30' VINEYARD VIXEN) "This family's favorite movie is 'The Quiet Man' and the leading characters' Irish cottage is named Inisfree. Inisfree also means loyalty, friendship, trustworthiness, etc…"

INNISFREE (34' TARTAN) "Jim and I and our wives considered hundreds of names. Because we consider our yacht our escape into another world, we named it after the 'Lake Isle of Innisfree' which is a mythical Celtic Shangri-la."

INSATIABLE (36' FRERS) "Ask my wife!"

INSTEAD (24' SEA RAY) "This boat is an 'elder-statesman', being built in 1977. In need of a lot of work, it appeared that all of my money was being spent on the boat instead of for food, shelter, and the education of my children. Thus, the name INSTEAD. All of the money was devoted to the boat instead of to the necessities of life."

INTERNATIONAL HARVESTER (42' PROVINCIAL) "I'm a lobsterman and the boat is used to harvest lobster and fish. We had her built in Prince Edward Island, Canada. She was constructed in Canada (INTERNATIONAL) and harvests lobster and fish (HARVESTER)."

INVIGORATOR (27' EVERGLADE) "We named the boat in honor of my grandfather, Lionel Price. Lionel was a WWII Purple Heart and Silver Star recipient. After the war, he owned a bar in Plain, Wisconsin called 'A Fair Price and a Square Diehl' with his relative Emil Diehl. He always referred to cocktails as 'invigorators', so after he passed away we wanted to name our boat something to honor him. Naturally, 'Invigorator' was a great fit!"

ISA LEI (43' COLUMBIA) "(Pronounced ESA LAY) I had made a trip to Fiji just prior to the purchase of our boat in the fall of 1972. The Fijians used the words 'isa lei' as a farewell. It was such a beautiful sounding word, I wrote to my friends in Fiji and asked for a definition and whether or not it would be appropriate to use as a name for our boat. While 'isa lei' has many meanings, the one that touched us most was 'a sigh of happiness'. She became ISA LEI in the spring of 1973, and indeed has provided many sighs of happiness."

ISLANDER (44' PETTEGROW EXPRESS CRUISER) "In keeping with the name of this classic down east cruiser, our family has enjoyed numerous trips to the islands of the New England coast and beyond."

WHERE THE WILD THINGS ARE

J ———

JACK TAR (19' RHODES) "Jack Tar was what English sailors were called in the age of sail. They always had tar all over them as it was used on the hemp rigging."

JAMES & CHRISTINE (32' MITCHELL COVE LOBSTER BOAT) "The boat is named after Michael's parents, James and Christine Cornell."

JANIE (35' C&C) "Our 3rd Janie. The first Janie was a Lightning class sailboat in 1957. At the time, we could not decide on a name. I was not fond of girl names, but our daughter was arriving at the same time of launch. Our daughter came first, so hence the name. It has been with us ever since in Marblehead Harbor."

JAZZ SANSATION (40' NELSON MAREK) "It began in 1981 when Saucony introduced a running shoe called the Jazz. I then called my next three boats JAZZ; a C&C 38LF, a C&C 38, and an Express 37.

Having bought the yacht SENSATION and wanting to adhere as much as possible to nautical tradition, rather than change the name of SENSATION, I just added the name JAZZ to it to keep my own 'heritage'. Following that purchase, my company then named a new spring '93 shoe, the Sensation…"

JEAN (16.5' TOWN CLASS) "This 'Townie' was named after my father's sister who has watched over our sailing endeavors since."

JEM (19' RHODES 19) "JEM represents the first initial of each of the three owners."

JESSLYN (25.5' GRADY WHITE) "The boat was named after our 2 girls, Jessica and Kaelyn."

JOE (17' FORESTER) "I asked my three year old daughter, Janie Grace, what she thought we should name the boat. She replied, 'JOE'."

JOHN CABOT (35' C&C) "We emigrated from Bristol, England. John Cabot was an explorer who left our homeport in 1497 and discovered America, landing in the Canadian Maritimes."

JOLI (19' RHODES 19) "This is the successor name to a previously owned wooden Town Class, which was more truly 'joli'...but this is also the first 2 letters in our first names...guess who?"

JOLLY GREEN (23' SEAWAY) "The topsides are dark green so our children, who were young at the time we bought the boat, named it JOLLY GREEN. They named it after the Jolly Green Giant of television commercial fame."

JOLLY KAY (19.5' O'DAY MARINER) "We got the boat shortly after my mother-in-law passed away. Her name was Katherine; Kay for short. Kay was always happy and jovial with friends and family. Therefore, it was only right to name our new boat the JOLLY KAY."

JOLLY MAN (27' PACIFIC SEA CRAFT) "Jimmy Buffet."

JUDITH F (9' ACHILES INFLATABLE) "Inherited the name when purchased at a yard sale."

JUDY SEA (28' HARRIS CUTTY HUNK) "My husband and I disagreed on whether it was supposed to be the wife's married name initial or maiden name initial, after the first name. He thought married, I thought maiden. My maiden name beginning with S and my married name beginning with C, it seemed appropriate to name her 'Judy Sea'."

JULIE ANN (27' CATALINA) "My little girl's name."

JUMPING JACK (27' SEA RAY) "I named it my nickname, which typifies my personality."

JUSTAJULE (34' FORMULA PC) "We had been trying to think of the name for some time, and were told by a dear friend, 'Don't worry, it will just come to you.' Well, we were at a party one night and I was talking about a prank I was going to play on someone, and another old friend looked at me and said, 'Julee, you are just a jewel.' A member of the group looked over and said, 'There's your boat name!'"

JUST COMICAL (22' CENTURY) "First syllable of the names of myself, my wife, and our two children, Alana and Justin. JUST-CO-MIC-AL (Justin, Connie, Michael, and Alana)."

K ——

KADUKA (28' CAL) "I got the boat. The kids got to name it. The name means; **A.** The ancient virgin goddess of sensuality. **B.** The Mediterranean term (expletive) for when the wind dies. **C.** The name of our cats. **D.** None of the above."

KAIKI (35' FANTASIA) "Hawaiian for 'new life'."

KANGAROO II (37' TARTAN) "Earnings from our freight transportation company Kangaroo Services, Inc. made it possible to purchase our sailboat. We thought it fitting to name it after the company. Our motto is, 'We're hopping to please you'."

KAPPYTAIN (24' WELLCRAFT) "Based on nickname."

KARAMEA (37' GULFSTAR SLOOP) "My father was investing in the stock market. He was given a tip on a New Zealand company and bought it cheaply. Within sixth months, it took off. He thought it peaked, so he sold it at a large profit which enabled him to buy the boat.

In honor of the company, he looked for a New Zealand theme. He chose to name the boat after Karamea Bay, off the northwest coast of the Southern Island."

KATABATIC (40' SAIL) "Katabatic is a meteorological term referring to a downdraft, as from a mountain or a glacier. Its opposite is anabatic, as in the thermal updrafts that eagles and hawks use to gain altitude.

When I bought the first of three boats by that name, the crew and I met to discuss a name for her. My excellent bowman, endowed with particular skill and agility, was coveted by other boats. He had just read a book about Antarctica and the fierce katabatic winds that blow down to the sea off the interior high land. He was so determined that Katabatic was the most appropriate possible choice, he declared he would not sail on her unless we adopted it. Case closed! It's turned out to be a good name."

KEEPER (23' MAKO SPORT) "I named the boat 'Keeper' because my husband is a Keeper. He is the Best!! He likes to think all fish caught will be Keepers!!!"

KEEP LOOKING (18'6" TYPHOON) "A friend told me because it took so long to find a name."

KEEP ON... (22' AQUASPORT) "Legacy mission statement from a Marblehead born T shirt company, founded by friends who had a collective inspiration to spread optimism by embracing a passionate & balanced life with an upbeat & energized attitude."

KESSELWASSER (31' RAMPAGE) "Kesselwasser translates to 'boiler water' in German. The other translation is a cocktail made of Pear Wilhelm and Martini. The owner has been in the boiler business for his career and has celebrated some orders with the drink!"

KHOKA MOYA (22.5' EDGEWATER) "Khoka Moya is a safari camp in South Africa. Jamie and I stayed there in October of

1994. Every day there was great and we think time on our boat is also great!"

KIRIN (28' J) "From Japanese folklore. A kirin is a Japanese mythical god. When one sees a kirin, good times and good fortune will follow."

KISMET 2 (35' BRISTOL) "During 1944, my family escaped by boat from East Prussia, when it was taken over by the Russians. We lived on that boat, KISMET (which means fate), for a year. My boat is KISMET 2."

KITTIWAKE II (44' BUNKER & ELLIS, 1964) "Kittiwake is a North Atlantic seagull who spends all year on the ocean. It is very hearty and also unusually dives for food. The name is original to the owner from Great Sprucehead Island, Maine."

KNIGHT OWL (32' C&C) "We wanted to use a bird because it flies on the wind and is graceful. We also wanted to incorporate our own name to personalize the boat.

The owl has been called the 'night watchman of our gardens' because it eats harmful rodents. This 'KNIGHT OWL' will watch over us while we are in our 'garden' at sea."

KNOTLESS (30' O'DAY) "Christ! Look at it!"

KRAZY KANGARUH (19.6' AQUASPORT) "The three of us were skiing in St. Anton, Austria and one afternoon, while sitting at an inn at one of the ski slopes, we decided to form a partnership to buy a boat.

The next summer when we bought our boat, we decided to name it in honor of the place where the idea was born; that inn in Austria – The Krazy Kangaruh!"

KUNGSORNEN (33.5' 1959 IOD) "She replaces the original Kungsornen dating from 1938, which was wrecked on a marine railway waiting to swell up one spring. The boats were all built in Norway. Hence a Norwegian name, which means King's Eagle."

KYAN (46' MORGAN) "A combination of the children's names, Kyle and Anne."

L ——

LADY B (35' CHRIS CRAFT COMMANDER) "I named it after my wife, Lady Bravos."

LADY JANE (17' GRADY WHITE) "After me."

LADY KELLEY (30' ETCHELLS) (The actual name of the boat is LADY SUSAN.) "In the summer of '89 I chartered an Etchells, USA 65, to race MRA and the Thursday Night Twilight Series. Kelley and I raced the Twilight Series together. I felt it was only appropriate to reflag the boat 'LADY KELLEY' for the summer.

One Thursday night late in August, I told Kelley we had to go out early because I had a spinnaker to look at for Doyle Sails. When she popped the kite, it had a proposal on it saying 'Kelley Marry Me. J.B.'. She accepted and the rest is history. We didn't race that night."

LADY SUSAN (31'6" TILLOTSON & PIERSON) "After wife."

LAGNIAPPE (34' TARTAN) "Lagniappe – a southern, French Cajun term means 'a little something extra'."

LA JOLLA (19.5' CORINTHIAN) "After a wonderful vacation in La Jolla, CA we returned to Marblehead and renamed our newly purchased boat."

LAST RESORT (40' C&C) "In 1975, the original LAST RESORT, an Ericson 35, was purchased. This name has a double meaning as the owner is in the travel business. When he purchased a new C&C 40 in 1979, he also named her LAST RESORT. She is green, which is also the company's color."

LAURENCE H. CONSTANTINE (35' NOVA SCOTIA LOBSTER BOAT) "Named after my grandfather, the late Lawrence H Constantine of Salem, MA."

LAURIE BELL (26' WINNINGHOFF) "Our work boat was named after Malcolm Bell, Jr.. 'Laurie' was an old Marbleheader, member of the EYC and BYC. For years, Laurie drove around in the old police boat with Dick Jodoin and, at one time, drove a launch at the Boston Yacht Club. Laurie died at the age of 68. He is missed by all of us at Jordan Marine."

LEGACY (33' PEARSON VANGUARD) "After having grown up on this boat for twenty three years, this son and his wife purchased the boat from his parents. The new owners felt that LEGACY was a perfect name for this boat as the history of this boat and the son's interest in sailing are both legacies."

LESLIE ANN (27' CATALINA) "Named after her 'owner' and avid sailor, our daughter."

LESS CHAOS (26' FORTIER) "We moved to Marblehead 17 years ago with three young children, and had a sign in our first home that read 'This House is Udder Chaos'. Very appropriate at that time. We named our first boat 'Rudder Chaos 14 years ago and now, as we wish our three (wonderful) kids off to college and careers, have named our new boat 'Less Chaos'. Great spot to spend quality time with family and friends."

LEVITATION (16.5' TOWN CLASS) "A play on Stan's name. The dinghy for this boat is GRAVITATION."

LIBATION (24' J) "Since I am a recent college graduate, I thought 'LIBATION' (a toast to the gods with spirits) was appropriate. The boat's dinghy is named 'LAST CALL'."

LIBERTY (26' OLD PORT LAUNCH) "The name came from the Barnegat Launch Service. A nice colonial name. We kept the name when we bought the boat."

LIFE OF RILEY (23' CHRIS CRAFT) "This boat was originally owned by Jim Reiley. Well known around the EYC and waterfront (both the boat and Jim), Jim was always helping the race committee run races. The boat was named 'RIGHT ON'. Jim eventually sold the boat to the EYC. The club used it and abused it for years as 'EYCRC'. They blew the engine in 1991 and pulled it. It sat just long enough with salt water in the engine to ruin it. So, we bought it for $1,000 – great deal!

Since everyone knew it as the old 'RIGHT ON' (Jim's boat), we figured it would be fitting to call it the 'LIFE OF RILEY' after the famous 1950 T.V. show, with the obvious play on RILEY/Reiley."

LIGHT WAVE (38' BARBERIS) "Our current boat came with the name. We like it. It's simple, self explanatory and evocative."

LILLE VENN (16.5' TOWN CLASS) "Lille Venn is Norwegian for 'little friend', a term of endearment in Norwegian. Our father-who was from Norway, used to call my mom 'Lille Venn' sometimes (It was his 2nd Norwegian nickname for her.). Our first Townie (1966) was called 'Vesla' (the other term of endearment).

Oddvar and Mary Ann (Mom and Dad) grew up sailing and on the water on opposite sides of the world. Mary Ann grew up in a house overlooking the San Diego Yacht Club and begged her dad to let her learn to sail. She was quite a racer in the 1940s! Oddvar grew up in Oslo, Norway and spent his summers as a child in the village along the coast. They met in graduate school in Massachusetts, and settled in Marblehead in 1964. Dad passed away in 2014. Mom can no longer sail and her two daughters and their husbands keep the Townie racing."

LIMERICK (33' C&C) "The former owner was from Limerick, Ireland."

LITTLE CLOUD (42' LITTLE HARBOR SLOOP) "We've been skiing at Snowbird/Alta in Utah since the late 70's and named our boat after our favorite powder runs at Snowbird!"

LIVE ANIMAL (20' TORNADO) "We found a kitten stranded on the Tinkers Island bell buoy. After rescuing it, we named her Tinker and the next boat, LIVE ANIMAL."

LIVING PROOF (17' BOSTON WHALER) "Living Proof is the name given to cancer survivors who ride in the Pan Mass Challenge, a 192-mile annual bike ride for cancer research and treatment. The boat owner is a 2-time cancer survivor and an 8-year PMC rider, so this was the perfect name to honor that history, and celebrate the joy that comes from boating in Marblehead."

LOLLYGAG (35' C&C) "Named after my daughter, Hadley."

LOLLY'S FOLLY (22.5' PEARSON ENSIGN) "Wife's name."

LOON-ATIC (34' EXPRESS) "The original name was LOON; a bit too staid and conventional. Given the combined personalities of the three owners, LOON-ATIC bubbled to the surface as being very appropriate."

LOOSE GOOSE (21' CENTER CONSOLE) "My father passed away 12 years ago and his CB handle was the Loose Goose. He was a big fisherman and he fostered my love of the water, thus the boat is named in his memory. He also was an avid hunter and loved hunting Canada Geese, thus his fondness of his CB handle."

LUCKY ESCAPE (20' LARSON) "On the day of its launch, we pulled out of our court and turned left down a hill. Unfortunately the boat didn't, as it had slipped off the trailer hitch. The boat was heading at speed towards a neighbor's brand new car! At the last moment, the boat struck the back of my car, coming to a rest and missing my neighbor's car by about one inch. Due to the angle that the boat hit my car, there was minimal damage to both boat and car. The same would not have been true if it had hit the neighbor's car. Hence the name!"

LUCKY TOUCH (43' SHANNON KETCH) "Our very first boat in South Africa (1970) was called LUCKY TOUCH and, as we have been 'lucky' with all the future ones, we gave our beautiful Shannon the same name: LUCKY TOUCH."

LUMBER JACK (22' SEA RAY) "Irving and Jack... own a lumber and building material business."

LUNA (21' ROTHBILT) "We only have a 21 foot boat so we had to keep it short. We thought about the name Moonstruck because we had the crazy impulse to buy our Rothbilt under the spell of a Harvest Moon. In the interest of brevity and perhaps copywrite infringement, we chose the name Luna. It's also the Spanish word for moon and so there's that added bonus."

LUPINE (38' FRERS) "We gave it the name. We have had other boats including a Concordia 41' sloop so named. Lupine is a spring wild flower common to the fields of Maine."

LYCKA TILL OCKSA (15.5' SNIPE) "This means good luck in Swedish. Previous boat was GOOD LUCK. This boat is used for racing."

LYRIC (32.5' ALOHA) "Over thirty years ago, we were searching for a name for our first boat, a Bullseye. One morning while reading the sports section of the Globe, we happened upon the horse racing results at Suffolk Downs which listed many horses with all sorts of names. One stood out, 'LYRIC', which we thought would be perfect for our new boat. We don't even remember if Lyric won her horse race, but we kept the name for our next boat, an Ensign, and carried it on to our present cruising boat. The tender for LYRIC is SEA NOTE."

GIRLS OF SUMMER

MAMA RHODA

MARBLEHEAD, MA

M ——

MACKINAW (28' ALBIN SPORT) "Our boat's namesake is the 1st icebreaker assigned to the Great Lakes. Prior to WW II, the US Government saw the need to keep the shipping lanes of the Lakes open in winter. The onset of the war made it imperative for the war effort. The 290 ft. Mackinaw, with a beam of 74 feet, was launched in March 1944. She home ported in Cheboygan, Michigan where she could quickly open the sea lanes in Lake Superior, Lake Huron, Lake Michigan and Lake Erie. This allowed for cargo ships carrying iron ore pellets to reach the steel mills.

Mackinaw USCG -83 was decommissioned in 2006. She is now on permanent display at the Icebreaker Mackinaw Maritime Museum in Mackinaw City. The new Mackinaw USCG-30 is a state of the art vessel capable of breaking through solid ice 32 inches thick. She is also doing duty as a buoy tender and for search and rescue missions. She is the guardian of the Lakes."

MAGGIE B (21' BAYLINER) "The name of my beautiful daughter."

MAGICEYES (26' CONTESSA) "My young daughter informed me she had 'magiceyes' as she could see things when sleeping."

MAGNOLIA (26' WASQUE) "Favorite flowing tree and, of course, 'Sugar Magnolia' is a great song!"

MAGURO (32' EVERGLADES) "The boat is named after what it's used to hunt for...bluefin tuna. Maguro is bluefin tuna in Japanese and is found on all sushi menus."

MAINE EVENT (36' DOWN EAST BHM) "The boat was built in Maine. It has a typical down east lobster boat hull with a yacht finish. I went to college at the University of Maine and fell in love with the area and people of Maine and decided to name the boat Maine Event."

MALACASS (22' CATALINA) "Our three children: Matthew, Laura, and Cassandra."

MAMA RHODA (38' EAST BAY) "For many years we went to CHUB CAY, an island in the Berry Islands of the Bahamas. We raised our girls going there every April for 2 weeks of fun in the sun, snorkeling, fishing, and beaching it. Just off the entrance to the Chub Cay Marina was a coral rock of pretty good size. It was probably 1/2 - 3/4 miles offshore. It was a place we loved to go and snorkel. It was a fun, beautiful place in the water that we looked forward to going back to every year. It was an easy place to get to and provided so much entertainment for us. When we sold our sailboat and bought our powerboat, we thought of 'Mama Rhoda' as a fun place out in the water that we loved going to. And that is our story!"

MAMBO TANGO (16.5' TOWN CLASS) "I purchased the boat without a name and searched for a name. Because the location for the name on a Townie is split by the rudder, I felt that a two word name was appropriate. Mambo Tango was the name of the raft used by Che Guevara to travel the Amazon in Colombia and I believe that the name was given to the raft because he really could not dance and his friends would say that he danced the Mambo Tango. I chose the name because I have Colombian family and I am not the best dancer."

M & EM (25' AQUASPORT) "Alden Hathaway, the uncle of the 2 girls the boat was named after, came up with this name as a combination of both of their names, Meagan and Emma. He took the 'M' from Meagan and the 'Em' from Emma, and combined them to make the M & Em."

MANDY (25' GENERAL MARINE) "Named after my father, William 'Mandy' Gillis; a Marblehead native and in the Marblehead Football Hall of Fame. Also, my late mother's (Katherine) store on Elm Street was named Mandy's."

MAN OF WAR (41' C&C) "Man of War, not Man o' War –the jellyfish, ironically ties back to Marblehead Harbor's early days. The man-of-war originated from the British Royal Navy as a name for a powerful warship/frigate from the 1500s – 1800s. (16th-19th centuries). How did it end up on our boat?

As our mother is originally from Yorkshire, England and our father served with the Marines in Korea, a British naval term seemed apropos. When my husband and father in-law purchased our C&C 41', there was no doubt that she was a powerful boat with classic lines and a strong racing history. She was a force on the water. In staying consistent with the British names from previous boats, they agreed upon Man of War. She now resides in Marblehead Harbor as did the USS Constitution, another man of war."

MANTICORE (44'6" LITTLE HARBOR) "We purchased MANTICORE, the first, in 1970. It came with the name. A manticore is a fictional animal with the head of a man, body of a lion, and the tail of a scorpion."

MANTON (17.5' MANTON SLOOP) "Manton is the name of the man who designed this boat. Built in 1945, this boat spent several years with the Marblehead Boat Rental Company and taught many Marbleheaders how to sail!"

MARA (28.6' ALDEN TRIANGLE, GRAVES, 1927) "Originally in Jamestown, RI. Purchased wreck on the beach 'as is' after the '38 hurricane. Called HOBBY because rebuilding her was the owner's hobby. Sold to Gloucester in the late 1940's. She was eventually purchased by a man whose wife wanted a chair. He called her WINGBACK. The triangle design was originally called the Marblehead One Design. When Marblehead finally became her home, she was called SHABUI (Japanese).

I call her MARA, a Swahili word with the nautical meaning 'a time'. Mar also means 'ocean' in various languages. MARA is short and sweet too."

MARBLEROSE (23' SEASPRITE) "We combined the names of the towns we both live in. David, from Melrose and Gary, from Marblehead – creating the name MARBLEROSE – something of beauty to last forever."

MARGARITAVILLE II (17' SILVERLINE) "Descendent of MARGARITAVILLE I, 1976. Named because of many Saturdays spent fishing, scuba diving and lobster trapping with friends, followed by chasing the women at Maddie's while tossing down Margaritas and listening to Jimmy Buffet on the jukebox."

MARLEN (34' J) "Len and Marie."

MARRY GIMBAL (17' SHAMROCK) "Just back from our honeymoon, Jack and I decided to meet some friends at The Landing. As soon as we arrived, our friends began to treat us to drinks. With each drink, everyone gave a toast of, 'Here's to the married couple!'

After rounds of toasts, Jack leaned over to me and whispered, 'Who is Mary Gimbal?' I broke out into laughter and told Jack that the toasts were for the 'married couple' and not 'Mary Gimbal'. When this group of friends all get together, we now drink to 'Mary Gimbal', whoever she may be!"

MARTA LYNNE (26' TIARA) "Named after our daughter."

MATCHMAKER (34' SEIDELMANN SLOOP) "In 1999, Sandra and I found each other on the new website 'Matchmaker.com', each of us having a love for sailing. In 2000, we got married, sold Sandra's 26 ft. Columbia 'Hiatus' and bought the Seidelmann, which was more suitable for extended summer cruising in New England."

MATILDA (18' WELLCRAFT) "This boat was named after the family dog."

MARTLET (22' SHAMROCK) "Our family has a history of naming boats after birds or animals. After a visit to our alma mater, McGill University, our grandson thought the fictitious birds called Martlets in the McGill coat of arms, made a perfect name for our new boat. The Martlet is a bird with feathers, but no feet. Never able to land, it flies on forever seeking knowledge."

MAVERICK (26' 1963 PEARSON ARIEL) "After extended debate as to whether the boat should be named after my wife, my daughter, or granddaughter, or a combination of all three; we all agreed to name it for the street we live on, as it seemed to reflect my attitude."

MEAN MONKEY (26' WELLCRAFT) "An old friend, Dwain Nugent, used to call my old girlfriend 'Mean Monkey'. A high-maintenance sport model. The same as the boat."

MEANDER (49' HYLAS) "We watched a boat wind through a narrow channel making a 'meander' and there it was. In retirement we plan to meander around."

MELANIE (28' SABRE) "Melanie was the first child born to Mark's sister. Since she was born the day before I bought the 19' Typhoon sloop, I named the boat after the baby.

I called Carol, a sign painter, to paint the name on the transom of my new boat. I didn't meet her, but she did a nice job. About a year later, I called Carol again to make posters for yacht club events. She made these posters for a year and a half and I still never met her. I asked her to lunch one Saturday (to make sure I would get the posters I needed). I asked her to marry me 15 days later! We were married 3 ½ months after we finally met 'face to face'. Together, we bought the current MELANIE. Guess who painted the name on it?"

MEMORIES (30' HUNTER) "Favorite singer is Barbra Streisand. Please note wife's name (Barbara). Favorite song is 'Memories'. Last boat was a Hunter 25.5 and also named Memories. Hence, when we purchased our new boat at the Newport Boat Show, the name naturally migrated to the new boat."

MERLIN (29' TRIPP VENTESCH) "My two daughters were fascinated with the tales of King Arthur. When we bought our boat, they immediately thought MERLIN was the perfect name."

MICBETH (27' TIARA) "A combination of our children's names, Michael and Beth."

MILLENNIUM (34' ALBIN) "We bought the boat at the turn of the Millennium and our kids were into Star Wars so we thought of naming it the Millennium Cod instead of Millennium Falcon. We ended up settling on just Millennium."

MILLIE 3 AND ME (17' HOMEMADE) "We've had three boats named MILLIE, after Mildred. So, the third one I named 'MILLIE 3 AND ME' after both of us."

MINDWELL (28' SABRE) "Mindwell is the middle name of the owner's daughter, Simone. This name originally came from a painting in Deerfield Village, MA. Simone's father thought that it resembled his mother-in-law!"

MIRAGE (32' BENETEAU) "French boat. Wanted a French sounding name."

MIRAGE (35' C&C) "We needed a name with even letters so it would fit on the transom and split the backstay. In desperation, as we were trying to document the boat, we tried about five names and finally hit MIRAGE and said, 'Way cool!'"

MIRLIN (25' SPORT CRAFT FISHERMAN) "My wife's name is Miriam and my daughter's name is Linda. So, I put together my wife's first three letters and my daughter's first three letters, and came out with MIRLIN. This is the second boat named MIRLIN owned by me."

MISIRLOU (40' 1964 CAL SLOOP) "50 years ago, the "California 40" earned fame as a revolutionary fast racing sloop in the "Trans-pac" race from San Francisco to Hawaii because it would actually "surf" down the face of huge pacific ocean swells. About that same time, California musician Dick Dale was known as the "king of surf guitar" and his signature, high energy surf music hit song 'Misirlou' was all over the airwaves. So, 1960's

California surfing boat named for a 1960's California surfing song, right? The Greek connection is also meaningful to our family since my wife and I spent our honeymoon and several anniversaries there."

MISS KNIGHT II (25' BAYLINER) "We had two elderly ladies that lived next door to us since 1965. Their names were Alice and Ruth Knight. When they passed away in the late 70's, they left each of the children $1,000 and my husband and I $10,000.

We always wanted a boat, so we purchased a small Regal and named it MISS KNIGHT. Then we upgraded and now have MISS KNIGHT II."

MISTAYA (29' BACK COVE) "We once went hiking in the Canadian Rockies in Mistaya Canyon, a beautiful place to be. So when we bought the sailboat, we thought we wouldn't be hiking in that area for a while but wanted to retain the memories. This is the second Mistaya."

MISTRESS (50' OFFSHORE LOBSTER & FISHING VESSEL) "My wife and I were married in February of 1961. At that time, I was having a 33' wooden lobster boat built in Maine which was launched in April of 1961. She claimed I cared more for the boat than I did for her (questionable). Hence, the name for the boat became MISTRESS. My present boat is the third one to have the same name. The relationship between boat, wife and me has always been constant!"

M. JULIP (21.5' RIGID BOTTOMED INFLATABLE RIBCRAFT 'RIB') "The RIB was built for the family in 2008 for the express purpose of chasing the kids around as they sailed their Optimist dinghies. As our fist Optimist, purchased used, was already named '007' and had a great set of bullet decals on the port and starboard sides near her stern, I thought a great name for the coach boat would simply be 'M' (James Bond's boss). My late wife, Rogina L. Jeffries (8/28/1959-11/11/2012), instantly replied, 'No that is not clever enough, you must name the boat to incorporate the children, Julia and Philip, and proclaimed: 'M. JULIP'.' Please note that M. JULIP should not be mistaken for Mint Julep, the drink. Also as a fun aside, since in Massachusetts you can choose the numbers and letters after the required MS of a motorboat registration, her official registration is: MS 2008 JP."

MO CHUISLE (25' GRADY WHITE) "A 'Chuisle mo chroi' means the pulse of my heart in Gaelic. When it is re-juxtaposed to 'Mo Chuisle' it loosely translates to my darling. This term was made popular by the movie, 'Million Dollar Baby', starring Clint Eastwood & Hillary Swank."

MOJO (27' SEA RAY) "Doug is an avid 'blues' fan and at-home guitarist. In the Negro Blues idiom, a 'mojo' is a good luck charm, such as a black cat bone. Because the blues was a direct precursor to rock-and-roll, some early rock songs refer to mojos. The most famous reference, perhaps, is 'Got My Mojo Workin'."

MOLLY WALDO (34' SABRE) "Named after a famous woman from Marblehead who saves a fisherman in the 1800's. Later, her name was used as a code name to respond to fisherman calling out in the fog for other fisherman."

MOON (34' WASQUE) "Named after a horse named Moon and also because the moon regulates the tides."

MOON SPINNER (32'6" VANGUARD) "Two of our former boats were named GEMINI for the space program and we wanted a moon-related name for this boat. At the time we bought it, we were going on a trip to Greece and read The Moon Spinners. We liked the legend of the Moon Spinners, a water nymph who spun the moon every month to let the creatures of the earth have a period of darkness. We think it is a lovely name."

MORNING LIGHT (23' STONEHORSE) "My great grandfather, Jacob Rogers, who went to sea before the mast at age 18, eventually owned half a clipper ship, the MORNING LIGHT. This was captained by his brother, Charles Rogers. The ship's name always appealed to me. Incidentally, I believe Jacob Rogers was one of the founders of the Eastern Yacht Club."

MORNING STAR (28' CAL) "It was on the boat when I bought it. I did a little research and discovered that Morning Star was a Northern Cheyenne chief, so I designed a logo where the left-hand part of the letter 'M' is in the shape of an arrow. I had a designer use a decorative font with a drop shadow that gives a 3D effect. Most people don't make the connection when they see it, but it looks great."

MORNING WATCH (30' PEARSON) "Shortly after we had purchased our sailboat, I happened to be walking through the Peabody-Essex Museum and saw the beautiful carving of a boat name that had been taken from the transom of an old sailing vessel called 'Morning Watch'. It struck me that this would be the perfect name for our boat as my husband and I both love the early hours of the day, and it is his favorite watch when sailing."

MUD HEN (30' NONSUCH) "She was the larger version of our first Mud Hen, a Crosby Cat. With generous sail and unique wishbone boom we sailed the New England coast for 23 wonderful years. We sold her, without the name in 2012. But, we are still the Mud Hen crew."

MULLIGAN (26' SISU) "Built and named in 2003 by Mary's parents, whose first love is golf. Mulligan was their 2nd retirement boat. Their first retirement boat didn't go well."

MUMBO JUMBO (23' SONAR) "Mumbo Jumbo is a 23' Sonar named after the Tufts University mascot, PT Barnum's elephant, Jumbo. Tufts sailors and other Tufts athletes are affectionately referred to as 'Jumbos'. Both father and daughter graduated from Tufts and often race in Marblehead's MRA and elsewhere with crew who were also Jumbos."

MUSCOBE (32' YOUNG BROTHERS LOBSTER YACHT) "This word, muscobe, was used by an Oklahoma cowboy friend in college 30 years ago to describe just about anything. A girl was a 'neat little muscobe' or a rodeo bull was a 'rank muscobe'. The word had no actual meaning but I told my friend, Duke Blackford, who is now a veterinarian, that someday I was going to have a big yacht in Marblehead and I was going to name her MUSCOBE. He never believed me until a few years ago when he came to visit. (This is actually MUSCOBE IV)."

MYSTERY (20' CENTER CONSOLE) "Got engaged on Madaket Beach in Nantucket. Celebrated with a few Madaket Mysteries, the house drink at the nearby Westender (now Millie's) Restaurant. Fond & fuzzy memories every time I see our boat Mystery."

MY THREE SONS (16' AMESBURY SKIFF) "Named for my three sons Devin, Malcolm and Connor."

ABC...1-2-3...

N ——

NALTEX (35' BRUCE ATKINS NOVI LOBSTER BOAT) "My children's names, Nate and Alex."

NANEPASHEMET (28' ALBIN) "Nanepashemet (died 1619) was the leader of the Pawtucket Confederation of Indian Tribes before the landing of the Pilgrims. He ruled over a large part of what is now Northeastern Massachusetts including the lands from the Charles River of present-day Boston, north to the Piscataqua River in Portsmouth and west to the Concord River. His name has been translated as 'New Moon'. Nanepashemet's tribe caught fish, dug shellfish and raised corn on the Marblehead peninsula."

NARNIA (27' CATALINA) "As third owners of this vessel, the name has stayed with her since her christening in1984. Based on the <u>Chronicles of NARNIA</u>, by C.S. Lewis."

NAUMKEAG (35' WEST SHORE MARINE TUGBOAT) "Naumkeag is the original name of Salem."

NAUSICAA (18' CATALINA CAPRI) "I named her 'Nausicaa' after a character in Homer's <u>Odyssey</u>. She was the daughter of the king and queen of Scheria (modern Corfu), the last island on which Odysseus was shipwrecked before his homecoming to Ithaca.

When he sets out from Scheria she says to him, 'Stranger, when you return to your country, remember that you owe your life to me.' It is one of the most charming episodes in ancient literature.

Nausicaa means 'burner of ships', or so I have read. I prefer to think that it is a contraction of 'naus kala', that is, 'beautiful little ship'."

NEREID (33' ALLIED; LUDERS) "In Greek mythology, the Nereids were daughters of Nereus, the sea god. They were sea nymphs. We liked that imagery for the name of our sailboat."

NEREID (23' ALBERG SEA SPRITE) "Nereid is the ancient Greek name for sea nymph(s). The boat is a Sea Sprite class vessel built by C.E. Ryder of Bristol, RI. Hence, NEREID."

NEVER AGAIN (31' TIARA) "I never thought I would buy another boat after selling mine in 2004."

NEVER BEFORE NOON (25' O'DAY) "Although most people who see our boat read other meanings into her name, the fact is with three kids and all the required paraphernalia, no matter how hard we try, we can never all get aboard before noon!"

NEW PRIORITIES (20' WELLCRAFT) "When asked if she'd babysit for two siblings of a one day old child (while the 'new' father was bringing the powerboat home to work on prior to launching in late May), the new grandmother explained that the boat could wait as the 'new' father had 'NEW PRIORITIES'! The boat came home before the 'new' mother returned from the hospital."

NIAM (28' MORRIS) "This name represents the owners, Nick and Amy."

NIGHTCAP (36' SHANNON VOYAGER DOWN-EAST CRUISER) "We used to cruise the coast of Maine and the Cape and islands each summer with my family. I can remember coming up to Nightcap (our family boat) as a teenager in my whaler and Dad was always on board tinkering. My Dad, Howie Jones, is the one who gave us the love of the water. We brought our kids up cruising and now we cruise with them and my siblings on our own boats each summer."

NIXIE (40' J) "This boat is named after the original NIXIE that was owned by my grandfather from 1898 to 1911. It was designed by E.M. Burgess and built in 1885. The original NIXIE can be seen today at the Mystic Seaport Museum."

NJORD (23' SONAR) "Norse god of the sea."

NOEY (21.5' PURSUIT) "My wife spells her name without an 'E'. It is Ann not Anne! When I married Annie my father was concerned on how he and the family would distinguish between his daughter Anne and my wife. So he asked her, 'Is there an E on the end of your name?' And she replied, 'No sir, there is no 'E' on the end of my name.' And everyone looked at each other and said, 'No E?' And so it began! Noey became her new nickname and all Clifford relatives call her that ever since."

NOMAD (38' SABRE POWER) "The boat name was on the first boat I purchased about 20 years ago and at the time I was in the moving business, so the name worked. Three boats later, we are enjoying cruising New England and the name still works."

NOMAD WIND III (38' LITTLE HARBOR) "Play on words. Double meaning."

NOMOR (35' C&C) "NOMOR is a fusion of Noah and Morgan, our two children's names. Susan devised the name. NOMOR(e) may also subconsciously reflect Susan's opinion of cruising. The name is problematic; if we buy a new boat, isn't 'NOMOR TWO' an oxymoron?"

NO NAME (19' BOSTON WHALER) "Worried that after naming the boat they would think of a better name."

NONPAREIL (32' C&C) "While antiquing in Vermont with family, we saw a painting of men and women with dogs in traditional hunting clothes titled "Nonpareil". We didn't know what Nonpareil meant, and asked our sister in law who was with us and has a French literature degree. She told us that "Nonpareil" translated from French means "without equal, or nothing better". Bingo! We thought what a great name for a boat. And so when we purchased our next boat, "Nonpareil" she was christened!"

NOON SOMEWHERE (12' MINI TWELVE) "The sun is over the yard arm…"

O ——

OBSEQUIOUS (22' 1974 CATALINA) "My daughter named our sloop. She wanted to spell it Obseaquious, however didn't tell her dad that there was a play on words. To her it seemed like the boat required constant attention and to own and care for it meant you need to be a servant to the boat and the rules of the sea. However, our boat brought our family together for long afternoons. It gave us a chance to experience harnessing the force of the wind. It allowed us to enjoy harbor illuminations and camp outs so we could be rocked to bed. Launching each year was a family ordeal and huge party night. Obsequious to the nth degree."

OCEAN SCOUT (20' OCEAN SCOUT) "Name of the manufacturer."

OCTOBER FOUR (43' BERTRAM CONVERTIBLE) "It is our wedding anniversary date."

OLIAIDE (36' SABRE EXPRESS) "I like to tell everyone that asks, that the boat is named for the 'Norse God of Giggles & Smiles'. Which is true. We named it for our 2 & 5 year old grandchildren, <u>Ol</u>iver and Ade<u>laide</u>."

ONE COOL REMOVE (31' GULFSTREAM TOURNAMENT) "When I bought my first offshore racing sailboat back in 1980, I knew even then that a time would come when I would switch to something else. After 30 years of sailboat racing and ownership of an additional 7 more offshore racing sailboats, I decided it was time for a change. I wanted something I could do with my wife that would not require a crew of 11 or so.

At the time, the Little River Band had a song out called 'Cool Change.' The song was about being out on the water. I decided this would be the name of my first power boat. However, I spotted the name 'Cool Change' on various water craft. This would not do. Then I discovered another song by Shawn Colvin called 'One Cool Remove.' It is a bit more esoteric and obtuse, but it still means a change from one thing to another…but without care as to what others may think. Hence boat No. 10: one Cool Remove, a powerboat from which I hope to learn about fishing…and , hopefully, catching."

ONTRO (23' CENTER CONSOLE) "I have used this boat's name on a number of previous boats. The name Ontro is for 'on the road'. O for 'on', T for 'the', and RO for 'road'. When out of my office (most sunny days) my secretary would say, 'I'm sorry. He's on the road.' Hence the name."

ORLANDO SON (36' BHM LOBSTER BOAT) "The owner has a son who moved to Florida and opened a lobster and restaurant business called the Bar Harbor Lobster Company. Since his son named the Florida company after a town in Maine, the owner felt it only appropriate to name his Maine built boat after a town in Florida."

OTTER (41' 1965 HINCKLEY SAILBOAT) "We named Otter for the creature that is happy in the water and later discovered that it was also the name of a ship owned by the family. Otter was well known in the Northwest fur trade and the China trade and was the first American ship to land in California (in Monterey), which at that time was Spanish."

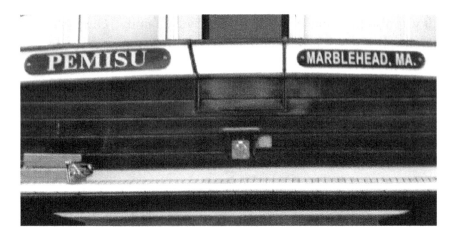

P ——

PADAWAN (17' BOSTON WHALER) "My 9-year-old daughter picked the name. My family are all big 'Star Wars' fans. A Padawan is an apprentice, or Jedi-in-training, who accompanies his or her master on missions. It seemed appropriate as it was our first boat, one we would all learn on. 5 years later we've been on many adventures with Padawan."

PAGEANT (37' TARTAN) "Family decision – derivation of our surname."

PAGURUS II (28' J) "Our daughter named our first boat PAGOO. The name was from a wonderful children's book of the same name, about a hermit crab named Pagoo. We owned and raced two Rhodes 19's with the same name. Our first cruising boat was purchased in 1978 – a Columbia 8.2. It was too big to be called PAGOO, so we went to the full Latin name for the hermit crab, PAGURAS. Much more dignified for a 27' boat. When we sold PAGURUS we bought a 22' Nonsuch. Cute, not dignified enough for PAGURUS, so back to PAGOO. In 1991, we sold PAGOO and bought our final hermit crab shell, the J28, and named it PAGURUS II. Like the hermit crab, we changed our shell 5 times as we got older."

PALMYRA (50' ABLE MARINE) "Named for the South Pacific Coral Atoll of Palmyra, of which I own a small part. I sailed this boat to Palmyra in 1987-1988; an 18,000 mile cruise."

PAMELA (42' GRAND BANKS) "As my previous three boats were, this one is named for my beautiful wife."

PANACHE (30' ETCHELLS) "It was the name of our prior boat, a C&C 30, that was lost in a Marblehead storm. The name 'Panache' denotes confidence and flair in the face of challenge. Thus, a fitting name for a race boat."

PARTNER'S CHOICE (30' DOWN EAST CRUISER) "Both my father and I were joint owners, 'partners', and we wanted a true Maine boat, a wooden one. We both enjoyed a little 'PARTNER'S CHOICE' ourselves during this joint venture."

PARTY PANTS (21' SEA STRIKE) "Because it's always a good day if you have your Party Pants on!"

PASSPORT (40' HINCKLEY) "Boat came with the name. Was named by previous owner who was allowed to buy the boat from his employer for forgoing a vacation for an emergency business trip."

PATRIOT (40' GULFSTAR) "This sailboat was designed by the late Ted Hood in 1977. I purchased it from Ted's nephew, Chris Hood, several years ago and never changed the name as it seemed fitting for a Marblehead boat of this vintage."

PEMAQUID (42' HINCKLEY SOU'WESTER) "We have owned her for over 14 years. She is named Pemaquid because my husband's ancestor, Ralph Blaisdell (the first Blaisdell from

Blaisdell, England), was shipwrecked on Pemaquid Point, Maine in 1635. The boat he was on was called the Angel Gabriel and the boat sank but Ralph managed to get safely ashore. That voyage was the beginning of the Blaisdell lineage in the United States. We named our boat in honor of that landing at Pemaquid."

PEMISU (47' GRAND BANKS) "Our family has owned numerous boats over the years, all named Pemisu. They have been on the same mooring in the middle of the harbor off BYC since 1956 and from 1949 off the CYC. My father named the boat Pemisu and explained that it was a Naumkeag Indian word for 'happy harbor'.

Naumkeag Indians settled in Essex County and the word Naumkeag means 'fishing place'."

PENNPACKET (TBD) "All boats that I own, have owned or will own solely are named PennPacket, because I am named after a sea captain, Peter Osborne, who sailed on the Pennsylvania Packet Ship in the 1770's. However, I do currently not own a boat solely."

PEREGRINE (32' ABLE WHISTLER) "Named for a desire to cruise, to travel…We cruise extensively to Canada, Connecticut, etc…"

PERIWINKLE (29' CHRIS CRAFT) "As a young child, my mother (who was from Holland), prepared periwinkles for snacks and I thought they were delicious. Also, I ski at Mad River Glen, where there is a trail named Periwinkle, and I have Periwinkle flowers in my garden. With these happy thoughts in mind, it seemed a natural progression to name my boat PERIWINKLE."

PFFT (26' RIVA AQUARAMA) "PFFT originally belonged to Victor Borge, the pianist and comedian. 'Pfft' is a phonetic name which, according to Mr. Borge, duplicates the sound of the boat passing by (Pfffffft)."

PHOEBE (38' TIARA) "New boat this year, named for me, the wife. 'Phoebe' was a fall back name as the family could not come up with 'something better'. BUT, I love having a boat named for me!"

PHOENIX (38' CUSTOM: J.O. BROWN & SONS, NORTH HAVEN, MAINE) "I had owned PHOENIX for two weeks and six days in October of 1976. She burned on Halloween, 1976 while hauled for a survey. A tank was leaking gas where a baffle had been welded. She was a total loss. I brought her home and spent three years in my driveway, rebuilding everything from the rails up, including the installation of two GMC diesels. Hence, she arose from the ashes as did the bird in Greek mythology. I look forward to the next 500 years."

PLAYIN' HOOKY (23' REGULATOR) "The Playin' Hooky is owned by a Marblehead teacher who is an avid fisherman. Upon purchasing the boat, his students suggested names and voted for their favorite. The class agreed that 'Playin' Hooky' brought both fishing and school together. The boat is now used to teach kids how to fish in the summer months."

PLAYPEN (19.5' AQUASPORT) "We bought the Aquasport the summer after our younger son, Jamey, was born. His sister, Kelly, was a few years older and just before nap time we'd all go out in the boat. The motion put them both right to sleep. The size of the boat made it a perfect 'play pen'. The name PLAYPEN is painted in alphabet blocks."

PLEIONE (8 METER SAILING YACHT) "The boat was built by the owner in his garage and launched in 2004. The very small transom required a short name. When Bruce was young growing up in Marblehead, he admired the New York 50 converted to a Schooner Rig named PLEIONE, owned by Joseph Santry for 30 years before being donated to the Mystic Seaport Museum. The Schooner PLEIONE was scuttled after Joseph Santry's death. I asked The Santry family permission to use the name and was granted permission. It is an honor to carry the name."

POCO LOCO (26.8' SEA RAY) "We're both a little crazy!!"

POINT OF VIEW (19.5' CORINTHIAN SLOOP) "As chairman of Marblehead Planning Board in 1988, when the boat was acquired, the name refers to then new zoning bylaw requirement to consider new development's impact on side yard view corridors when viewed from the water and not just from adjacent streets. My search for a boat was jokingly referred by some as a need for a 'planning board police boat'."

POLLY B (42' GRAND BANKS) "From my wife's name."

POMPANO (33' IOD) "A pompano is a fish. This is the original name of the boat."

POSSUM (17' WHALER) "Named after a cute, innocent girl whose nickname was 'possum'."

PREAMBLE (32' MORGAN) "In Feb. 1990, while I was in command of the USS CONSTITUTION, I purchased our current boat. My wife and I were busily searching for a meaningful name as the deadline to document the boat with the Coast Guard was rapidly approaching. We even purchased a book of names for boats. My son John said, 'Dad, why not name her PREAMBLE since you will be keeping the boat alongside OLD IRONSIDES?' Thus, it was proudly named PREAMBLE."

PRINCE ODIN (22' BOSTON WHALER) "I bought the boat from a man in Plymouth, Mass., who instructed the ship's carver to inscribe it as the PRINCE EUGENE, named after the famous battleship of the German Navy. The carver couldn't spell right, so it came out PRINCE ODIN.

This is one of the original 'Outrage' series of boats developed by Boston Whaler (#0060)."

PRIZED COD (22.2' AQUASPORT) "The owner won the 'Governor's Trophy' for catching the 'prized cod' that year."

PROMISE (40' J) "The boat had that name when I bought it."

PUMPKIN (12' BEETLECAT) "This is my second Beetlecat. The first was named LADYBUG, after my father's sister's Beetlecat. My new cat is PUMPKIN because of the shape of the hull (a bit squat), the color of the canvas deck (a squash color traditionally done by the builder), and because it is my nickname for my three year old who is now old enough to go sailing with me. (We have a five year old too.)"

Q ——

QUADRILLE (42' ALLIED XL II) "QUADRILLE was ordered by my father and Nelson who were in as partners. In the summer of 1970, she was launched for her maiden voyage. A great success! My parents and Nelson and his wife, sailed QUADRILLE from Mystic, CT to the St. John River. As there were four people and a French dance involving four people called Quadrille, the name was picked."

QUADRUE (19' RHODES 19) "The name had to be seven letters with one that repeats for good luck. There are also four owners, so we came up with QUADRUE, which is sort of a prefix meaning four."

QUERENCIA (16.5' TOWN CLASS) "William F. Buckley, an American author, wrote that 'querencia' doesn't really translate to English, but is used to 'designate that mysterious little area in the bullring that catches the fancy of the fighting bull when he charges in. He imagines it his sanctuary: when parked there, he supposes he cannot be hurt...So it is, borrowing the term, that one can speak of one's 'querencia' to mean that little, unspecified area in life's arena where one feels safe, serene.' Buckley wrote this in his book, Racing Through Paradise, which was published in 1988."

QUEST (33' BOOTHBAY) "Quest for the sea. My previous boat was named QUEST. I liked it!"

QUICKSILVER GIRL (31' BERTRAM) "Name of a song my wife and I liked while in college."

HAPPY HOUR

R——

RAGE RAGE (40' PALMER JOHNSON) "It is named from a line in a poem by Dylan Thomas. 'Do not go gentle into that sweet good night, but rage, rage against the dying of the light.'"

RAVELLO (20' ENSENADA) "Named after Ravello, Italy, one of the most beautiful towns on the Amalfi Coast."

RAW BAR (13' SAILING DINGHY) "Presented to me as my wedding gift. Peter placed the boat all set up underneath our wedding tent, the eve of our wedding.

I had planned a raw bar for the wedding and needed a boat in which to place the seafood. Peter assured me that he had this under control. Sure enough, after he gave me my present, it reappeared the next day in full sail, on the lawn as a raw bar. Yum!"

RECESS (16.5 TOWN CLASS) "Named because Laurie is a first grade teacher at Bell School in Marblehead and the boat to her, is analogous to recess for her children."

RECESS (30' 1970 CORANADO) "She was originally named Daystar-II. We purchased her in 1999 from a friend in Salem and moved her to our new mooring in Marblehead, just off the MYC dock. In 2011, we reconditioned the hull and in the process renamed her 'RECESS' to commemorate my wife's 25 years of teaching kindergarten at the Gerry School in old town."

RECON MISSION (13' BOSTON WHALER) "Since this Whaler is used to explore and search for prime locations to put lobster traps, every trip is a Recon Mission."

REDBIRD (26' MACKENZIE CUTTYHUNK) "The hull is painted a bright red."

REEL TIME (28.5' MAKO) "Thought the catch on word says a lot. True please of fishing and enjoying the moment for it all happens when you step on the boat."

REMEDY (25' POWER) "'Remedy' is the best song from The Black Crowes! And, being on the boat in and around Marblehead Harbor helps forget all that ails its passengers."

RENAISSANCE (35' SPARKMAN & STEPHENS) "My wife and I were married in 1987. Because it was a second marriage for both of us, this was a time of renewal and new beginnings. RENAISSANCE seemed like an appropriate name for the boat we bought together."

REVERIE (34' TARTAN) "We had a 'Name Pool' with friends from home and work and out of all the choices that we got, this one closely matched what we have in mind when out on the water. 'Reverie – state of dreamy meditation or a day dream'."

RIBIERAS (16.9' O'DAY DAYSAILER) "Named after a parish on the island of Pico, in the Azores. My mother's father has Portuguese roots spanning 300 years."

RIPPLE (24' AQUASPORT) "Named after the song by the Grateful Dead."

RISING SUN (32' JARVIS NEWMAN) "My boat is used for commercial lobstering. When it was being built, I looked at an old book which listed names of many of the old fishing schooners that fished out of Marblehead during the late 19th century. Most of these vessels were named after wives or daughters, but several were flashier."

RIVAL (38' TAYLOR SLOOP) "The boat was custom designed by Marblehead's Jim Taylor for the previous Gloucester owner. Rival was named after another Rival, a B.B. Crowninshield schooner which was owned by the father of Rival's current owner."

ROARING BULL (36' JARVIS NEWMAN) "While growing up in Marblehead, the Roaring Bull spindle lined up with the owner's front door. (The owner's father used to have a boat that was also named ROARING BULL)."

ROCK STAR (38' EAST BAY) "Our J105 was originally named STAR EYES. We changed that to SHOOTING STAR and campaigned her successfully for 5 years, before selling her. When we purchased the East Bay, names got tossed around and we decided to stay with the 'Star' theme. We are not crazy about the name ROCK STAR.

After selling our J105 we purchased a J100 and named her ILLUSION. 'Illusion' is a ski trail on Bear Peak at Attitash Mountain in Bartlett, NH. It is a great top to bottom run. The J100 has been sold, so we have become 100% power boaters."

ROK-IT-SHIP (29' BACK COVE) "Our last name is Kurzrok and we often call ourselves the Roks. We came up with many variations: On the Rocks, Rock and Roll, and others, but they all seemed to remind us of unpleasant boating days or unpleasant experiences. Finally, we thought of 'Rok-It Ship' and it seemed to fit."

ROLL 'EM (30' ETCHELLS) "This name is a play on words, as the sail number is 711 (great when gambling) and this boat handles the rollers on the ocean well."

ROSEBUD (35' TEKTRON CATAMARAN) "From the sled in the Orson Welles film, 'Citizen Kane'. The sled was a symbol of the joys of being a child in nature that no amount of wealth and power could duplicate."

ROVER (20' ANSWER) "All of the cousins tried to come up with a good name for this boat. After weeks of trying, no one could agree to a name. Jack Sheperd (10 year old cousin) said, 'Oh, why don't you just name it ROVER?' And name it ROVER we did!"

R2D2 (20' GRADY WHITE) "My initials are RR. My better half's initials are DD. It was a no brainer."

RUBBER DUCK (9' ACHILES) "When this boat floats around on the water, it resembles a rubber duck."

RUFFIAN (40' J120) "My wife was an equestrian who converted to sailing. She selected the name Ruffian in honor of the race horse. Ruffian (April 17, 1972 - July 7, 1975) was an American champion thoroughbred racehorse. Ruffian was ranked among the top U.S. racehorses of the 20th century by The Blood-Horse magazine. Within one short year she would establish herself as one of the greatest racehorses to set foot on the track. She won her first ten starts with ease, the perfect champion. But she would never finish her 11th race. Ruffian's eleventh race was run at Belmont Park on July 6, 1975. It was a match race between Ruffian and that year's Kentucky Derby winner, Foolish Pleasure. The flawless filly, the hometrack hero, would break down in the stretch during one of the most anticipated match races of all time, proving that only death could defeat Ruffian's great thoroughbred heart."

RULEDA (30' SPARKMAN & STEPHENS) "This is named after the owner's wife and two daughters."

RUNNING FREE (37' TARTAN) "Many years ago in the 70's, at a Club Med in Guadeloupe, we sailed Lasers in a group of 10-15 boats, with a French speaking 'GO'. After an hour of beating, miles away from the Club, he would call in a French accent, 'rrunning frree!!!' We would turn back, pull center boards out and RUN FREE! That exhilarating feeling and experience has always stayed with me. My wife and kids loved the name RUNNING FREE!"

RUSTLER (37' EXPRESS) "After disagreeing about many names for the boat, the three co-owners finally agreed on naming it after one of the most famous ski trails in the world, and one of our favorites: 'High Rustler', at Alta, Utah."

RYAN II (26' PEARSON) "My belated husband, Richard, named the boat after our daughter, Ryan, on 8-25-82."

S ——

SABRINA (42' SABRE) "Sabrina is the name of the witch on Bewitched played by Elizabeth Montgomery. Sabrina is a Sabre 42 which we had built in 2012. Since Sabrina also has a black hull, we decided to go with the witch theme for this boat."

SAILMAN (30' S-2 9.1) "I am a salesman and wanted to make an excuse that I was not in work, but with another salesman."

SAINT JUDE (30' SABRE) "Named after a loved Beatles song which also includes the owner's name."

SALACIA (35' FREEDOM) "The name is of Neptune's wife, the goddess of salt water. My wife had a cousin with a boat named Neptune. When we chose the name, I had a friend doing her doctorate in mythology at Harvard. I asked her if there were any bad connotations to this goddess. After some research, she reported that there were not. The high speed catamaran that runs from Boston to Provincetown is also named Salacia. The boat sails out of the Marblehead Yacht Club."

SALTY (20' PACIFIC SEACRAFT – 'FLICKA') "Because she gets salty from ocean spray in heavy weather and she has a traditional salty look. A cruising cutter rigged for single handed sailing with additional rigging for a physically challenged sailor."

SALTY FOX (24.5' AQUASPORT) "1995 Horribles Parade entry float of a 'ship' the children named the Salty Fox."

SAND DOLLAR (34' NOVA SCOTIA FISHING BOAT) "When lobstering aboard this boat, the 'catch of the day' seemed to usually include many sand dollars. As a result, a sand dollar collecting hobby and a thirst for the knowledge of the various sand dollar legends were begun."

SANTOSA (26' FORTIER) "Santosa= contentment."

SARAH (24' CUSTOM LOBSTER TYPE) "Wife's name."

SCALAWAG (23' MAKO) "Named after my son, Ben."

SCARLET FEVER (30' REDWING) "It is red."

SCHUSS (22.2' AQUASPORT) "We are a big skiing family in the winter. 'SCHUSS' just seemed a perfect name for a boat that went fast!"

SCHWENDI (36' SABRE) "I have taught skiing at Waterville Valley for over 40 years on the weekends. In fact, I met my wife there. The name of the warming hut at the top of Waterville Valley is called the 'Schwendi Hutte'. It is where everyone goes to get a hot chocolate and a warm, fresh-baked cinnamon bun in the mid morning. Over many years, we got used to taking a 'Schwendi break' on those cold winter mornings to get re-energized.

Now we can take a 'Schwendi' in the summers as well!"

SCREAMIN' EAGLE (23' SEACRAFT) "Co-owners and wives are all graduates of Boston College, so we appropriately named our boat after our beloved alma mater. We incorporated the logo in the same style as one of the BC logos as well."

SEADOZER (21' OCEANIC) "My husband's business is heavy construction. The bulldozer is the standard of the heavy earth moving industry. Hence, the off-time pleasure with the SEADOZER."

SEADUCTRESS (25' ERICSON) "We can always hope!"

SEA FEVER (36.2' SABRE) "Our boat is named Sea Fever, after the John Masefield poem of the same name. My wife grew up sailing Long Island Sound on her family's Seafarer 23 Kestrel that was also named Sea Fever. She wanted the same name for our boat. So we agreed that she could name the boat and I could name our two children. Fair deal."

SEAESTA (34' POWER) "My grandmother, Esther, was a force of nature. As a Bostonian, she was often called 'Esta'. Throw in the Spanish word siesta and there you go!"

SEA FLEA (34' NOVI LOBSTER BOAT) "I used to fish off an offshore fishing boat named SEA DOG, owned by Roger Bakee of Marblehead. When I got my boat in 1984, I decided to call it SEA FLEA because I'd never seen it and besides, my wife didn't want it named after her."

SEA HOUND (28' BERTRAM) "The name came from a dog, which is a Ridgeback (or a hound)."

SEA LEGS (29' PURSUIT SPORT FISHERMAN) "I named it after the original SEA LEGS, a 54 ft charter boat, owned by Loyd Hendricks, which I ran for several years. I found the boat on EBAY and it was located in Georgia. Despite what everyone told me, I went ahead and purchased it. Everyone said, 'It's a mistake since it was on EBAY and must be a piece of junk.' But I surprised everyone. Now they say that all I do is fall into deals."

SEA LODGE (26' POWER) "When I bought the boat I was living in a 300+ year old house which had been a Tea House in the 1930's. Today the house is still known by its Tea House name – 'The Spruce Lodge'. My mother told me to name the boat 'Sea Lodge'. Who wouldn't take advice from their mother?"

SEAMARK (8.3 METER GRIADI) "Seamark is a fish importing company that was located in Boston. The VP of sales went to Denmark and had the boat built to his specifications. The boat was used for customer entertainment and pleasure. In 1992, the company suddenly went into Chapter 11 bankruptcy. I bought the boat from the bankruptcy court."

SEA NOTE (8' ROW BOAT) "As a tender to LYRIC, we bought a row boat for $100. In keeping with the musical theme, and to recognize the cost, we named her SEA NOTE."

SEA OTTER (18' NOWAK AND WILLIAMS) "The boat was designed by Don Arnow, the designer of cigarette boats. Sea Otter was the name of the model of the boat. We purchased it in 1975. At that time we couldn't agree on names: 'Out to Launch' (it looked like a yacht club launch even though it will go 29 knots) or 'Shake and Bake' (the boat was a French's mustard yellow) somehow didn't seem quite right. So, over the years, the Sea Otter became known as the Sea Otter."

SEAPAM (26' BRISTOL) "The four members of our family have the initials M.A.P. Backwards it spelled P.A.M. Thus, our Bristol 26 was named SEAPAM."

SEA PAWS (34' C&C) "The boat was named after a sailing cat named Sea Paws."

SEA PONY (42' GRAND BANKS) "Mystery name."

SEASONS PASS (28' LEGACY) "We are a family of skiers....we loved the double meaning..."

SECOND WIND (30' NONSUCH) "When we bought the boat in 1987, I had recently joined a new firm after fourteen years in a firm that had to be closed. It was a fresh start. Also, after 20 years of racing around the buoys in a Shields, we decided to stop racing and start cruising. A new way to sail."

SEEHUND (19' DELLQUAY DORY LAUNCH) "Prior to our purchase, this boat was 'SKOLDPADDA', which is Swedish for 'turtle'. Having no Swedish connection and noting that the boat is English with a Norwegian engine, we felt no compunction to retain that name. Instead, having a German background, we chose the name SEEHUND which translates literally to 'sea dog' but which is the German term for a 'seal' – which the boat, having black topsides, strongly resembles not only in appearance, but also in character."

SEGUE (45' FREEDOM) "Segue means to transition. Our boat will transition us to a new lifestyle."

SEYON (65' CUSTOM JACK HARGRAVE DESIGN) "SEYON is named after the many other boats of the same name owned by the Noyes family. SEYON is Noyes spelled backwards. The original SEYON was owned by Mr. Harry K. Noyes and then his son continued the tradition when he bought his wife a powerboat by the same name for her to watch her children race. This SEYON was also used by the Race Committee for the America's Cup. The current SEYON was originally built for one of the CEO's of Coca-Cola and features many unique elements related to the soda. Even the boat horn's handle is a miniature wooden Coke bottle."

SGIAN DUBH (22' SHAMROCK) "The words 'sgian dubh', pronounced (skeen-do), are Gaelic and mean 'black knife'. It is the small weapon carried in the sock when wearing kilts. Called a black knife because it was, in early days, a concealed weapon."

SHADOW (22' LAUNCH) "The name came as a result of the fact that it is a smaller launch than the other launches owned by West Shore Marine. Hence, SHADOW."

SHALLOW UP (26' PACEMAKER) "The genesis of the boat name 'Shallow Up' is derived from the adventure writer Randy Wayne White's series of Doc Ford novels. Most his stories surround the activities and adventures of Doc Ford and his sidekick Tomlinson in the Southwest Florida water areas of Sanibel Island, Captiva Island, Cayo Costa Island and Pine Island. 'Shallow Up' is a term that Tomlinson uses in several of White's novels when he and Doc are in tight situations with bad guys all around them, and Tomlinson is trying to get Doc to relax and take it easy. 'Doc, shallow up man, relax, everything is going to be OK.' Also, our boat is moored in the back end of the harbor. This area is referred to by many as the 'shallow' end of the harbor."

SHEA'S LOUNGE (18' PRECISION) "Many years ago we had a small sailboat which I named ROOD RUDDER. When I bought this newer one as a gift to Shea, I thought and thought to try to think of something catchy, and all of a sudden it came to me clearly. Since Shea is my husband's first name, and since sailing should be relaxing, which is what a chaise lounge is used for; I knew it just couldn't be anything else but SHEA'S LOUNGE."

SHEPARD (26' FORTIER LAUNCH) "Named after the original founder of West Shore Marine Services, Eric Shepard."

SIDEKICK III (30' ETCHELLS) "I think you can guess! (This is a play on words from the owner's last name)."

SIDELINE (24' GRADY WHITE) "I think you can guess! (This is a play on words from the owner's last name. The owner's other boat is called SIDEKICK III)."

SILKIE (41' TARTAN) "SILKIE comes from Scottish folklore. The 'silkie', is a seal that comes ashore and takes the form of a man. He then seduces the Scottish women and when the children grow up, he returns and claims them back."

SIMBA (18' CAPE COD CATBOAT) "My first boat, when I was ten, was a Beetlecat (12') in Nantucket. 'Simba' is Swahili for lion. Lions are cats, so my Catboat became SIMBA. She, in 1928, was the first of five SIMBA'S."

SINE QUA NON (30' ETCHELLS) "This is a Latin term roughly meaning, 'If you aren't sailing this boat, you are nothing.' (The current owners inherited this name.)"

SIROCCO (41' FRERS) "Opposite wind of the mistral, which was the name of my father's boat."

SKAL (22' SPORTCRAFT) "A family name handed down over generations. A 'toast' meaning 'bottoms up'."

SKI BREAK (22' SEA RAY) "I named my boat SKI BREAK because our family ski's during the winter and since we can't ski in the summer, we call boating a 'ski break', or just a breather from a winter pastime."

SKIDDER (21.5' AQUASPORT) "'Skidder' is the name of one of our favorite trails at Sugarloaf in Maine. A skidder is a machine used to drag logs to the river."

SKIMMER (33' BERTRAM) "This boat is very fast and low to the water. It appears to 'skim' along the ocean."

SKOL (19' MAKO) "Swedish for 'cheers'! (Or so I thought.)"

SLOOP DOGG (26' PEARSON) "The wife thought of it. It stuck. She has regretted it since."

SMALL HOTEL (33' IOD) "Second SMALL HOTEL. Raced competitively in Marblehead water 1970-2006. Name comes from the flag alphabet H. The original owner bought 8 wood IOD's, new from the only original builder in Norway, Bjarne Aas', around 1954 on Long Island Sound for training purposes. His personal boat was the last one, H, which he named SMALL HOTEL. Most of the 8 migrated to Marblehead but none under the alphabet names. New owners in 2006, but still racing competitively with same name."

SMOKE (38'5" SOVERAL) "Inherited."

SNAPPY (15.5' SCOUT) "Because it is a snappy little boat!"

SNATCH BLOCK (23' SEA OX) "This is the owner's nickname. He was born in an apartment at Graves Lower Yard. At that time, all of the boats were lifted in cradles held by 'snatch blocks'. As a child, he could never say 'snatch block' correctly, so his friends bestowed upon him the nickname."

SNOW DANCE (45' FASTNET) "Being in the ski industry, a 'snow dance' is what these boat owners do all summer long in the hopes of guaranteeing a snowy winter!"

SOLILOQUY (33' BRISTOL) "Tranquil and peaceful. A place to be relaxed."

SOUTHERN COMFORT (25' C&C) "I bought it in 2008 without looking at the name. It turns out that the drink Southern Comfort was my mother-in-law's favorite. The boat was duly christened by my wife and her sister, with a round of Southern Comfort on the rocks."

SPARTINA (19' SEAWAY) "Sea grass."

SPELLBOUND (27' CATALINA) "An obvious choice being in such close proximity to Salem, MA with its witches and their 'spells'. Was I telepathically directed to choose this name?"

SPIRIT (30' ERICSON) "In 1991, SPIRIT, then CRYSTAL, lay in a Newburyport yard. She was suffering the effects of being outside since she was wrecked in Hurricane Gloria in 1985. Her owner did not have the time to complete repairs he started many years ago. She was in a sorry state.

I had just gone through an ugly divorce. The boat was just what I needed to give me hope for the future and help mend my 'spirit'. She certainly did the job well, so we named her SPIRIT."

SQUASHBLOSSOM (32' REVEL CRAFT CABIN CRUISER) "American Indian necklaces."

STACEY H. CLARK (31' JC) "This boat is named after the first Marblehead Harbormaster!"

STARRY NIGHT (42' SABRE) "Starry Night was named to represent the junction of two passions; my wife's love of the arts, she a painter, and my love of the ocean and its creatures, myself an avid scuba diver.

You see, when we were married, the folks at the New England Aquarium, where I work, sponsored a Right Whale in our name as part of the right whale research program. The many white scars and dots on the whale's black body reminded researchers of the night sky and so named her Starry Night. Starry Night of course, is one of Van Gogh's best-known works. The painting Starry Night, painted in June 1889, depicts the view outside of Van Gogh's sanatorium room window in southern France at night."

START ME UP (17' MONTAUK) "I always felt it was the perfect name for a sporty center console powerboat. I had the name picked out years before we got the boat."

STEELAWAY (19.5' CORINTHIAN) "Dual meaning: I am from Pittsburgh, PA, 'The Steel City'. The boat is used for One Design racing. We steal a win now and then!"

STILL KRAZY (21.5' SEA SWIRL) "Prior boat was named 'Krazy Kanguruh' after the well known Austrian ski bar. After selling that boat, my new one is 'Still Krazy'."

STORMALONG (29'11" C&C) "Stormalong was a real boy cadet, on Alan Villiers' ship JOSEPH CONRAD. He appears as a hero in the book, STORMALONG, by Alan Villiers. My wife Sally first used the name on her 110 in Long Island Sound, 1948-1949. We also named our 210 #363, STORMALONG (1965-1976), before the C&C in 1980."

STREGA (46' J) "We had the boat built in 2004. We decided it would have a black hull. One night when we were at dinner at the Strega restaurant in Salem, it occurred to us that Strega (witch in Italian) would be a good name for the boat. Witches are associated with black and the letters in Strega look nice in lower case, which is how they are painted on both sides of the hull."

STRIKE OUT (AVON) "Tender to Home Run. We subsequently named our Avon inflatable "Strike out" because when cruising, we strike out from Home Run to visit islands and towns."

STRIPER II (30' FORTIER) "From the STRIPER skippered by one of the best charter boat captains in Cape Cod Bay from 1945 to the mid 80's, by the name of Joe Eldridge. I worked on and also skippered his STRIPER from 1952-1958."

SUERTE VERDE (16.5' TOWN CLASS) "JB and I have been looking at the 'Townie' as a good boat for me for about 20 years. It is a classic boat! And, a great boat to learn in with a growing fleet and very supportive members. I did not grow up sailing and have felt that in order to really learn, you need to be in a little boat. As a Christmas present, JB gave me my own boat! He figured to really learn, it was time for me to get on a boat by myself and figure it out! To name the boat, we wanted something Spanish because of our time living in Valencia. We liked the deck top color, a teal green. And, I am of Irish decent. So, 'Suerte Verde' which translates as 'green luck' or the 'luck of the Irish'. 'Green' because I am a new sailor and 'suerte' for luck, because I feel lucky and because you need a little of it!"

SUMMER SCHOOL (22' EASTERN) "We use this 'Summer School' to motivate scholastic performance. They don't want the alternative…"

SUNDAY SILENCE (22'J) "This was a winning race horse at the Kentucky Derby."

SUNDOG (23' PROLINE) "We originally had a 21' Aquasport. The engine died and instead of repowering the boat, we traded it in and bought a new one. I had been asked to play hockey for a minor league start up that longtime friends were running. The team name was the Arizona Sundogs. I graciously declined as a result of being a father of two very young children, who was also employed in our family business. Sundog seemed like a good fit."

SUNFISCH (17' SEA HUNT) "The name is a play on words with our last name. Our daughter's Opti was SAILFISCH."

SUNSHINE DAYDREAM (27' GRADY WHITE) "I had this name in mind for a boat, going back 20 years, as part of my love for the Grateful Dead. I always said that when I bought my first boat, she'd be named Sunshine Daydream. In 2007, I kept my word."

SUPERFINE (34' PEQUOD) "We bought the boat while employed by Mohawk Paper Mill, and the top grade of paper we manufactured was Superfine. We have owned her for 29 years, and she is now 41. She is a fiber glassed lap strake boat with a modified v hull and has a 12 ft. beam. We feel she is worthy of her name. The boat is a Pequod and was built in Concord, N.H. They were built from 1972 to 1983, all one size and she is a 1973.

SUSAN MARGARET (32' COVEY ISLAND LOBSTER BOAT) "When our boat was being built, my wife said, 'That's my first house. You'd better name her after me!'"

SYBARIS (32'1" BRISTOL) "Sybaris, an ancient Greek city in southern Italy, was populated by folks who appreciated the 'good life' of luxury and pleasure. Harmony was the rule of the day. Sybarites are known for their hedonistic approach to life."

SYNERGY (30' SHIELDS) "Last owner was an engineer."

T ———

TAANUGI (19.5' O'DAY MARINER) "TAANUGI sounds somewhat Japanese, but is actually the Hebrew word for 'my pleasure'."

TALLADY (40' BRISTOL) "Wife is 6'."

TAMBOURINE (21' CATBOAT) "We named our Catboat TAMBOURINE because it is so round and we keep throwing money in to maintain it safe and sound. You never hear a sad song played on a tambourine, so I think the name's appropriate. So do Adam, David, and Irene."

TANGO (33' IOD) "The name came with the boat."

TAYGETA (41' NIELSON CUSTOM) "Taygeta is one of the Pleiades, a group of stars in the constellation Taurus. They are referred to as the 'Seven Sisters', and in Greek mythology are the daughters of Atlas and Pleione. Both 'PLEIONE' and 'TAYGETA' were names of yachts in my wife's family."

TECUMSEH (32' HOLLAND LOBSTER BOAT) "Tecumseh was the name of my father's first boat, which was a popular racing class in the 40's and 50's, called the Indian. Tecumseh was an Indian Chief. Therefore, the name. We resurrected it!"

TEN (45'3" BRISTOL) "It's the 'PERFECT' boat!"

TENDERLY (23' SEA CRAFT) "Owned by my lovely wife as a tender for my Etchells."

TEST RUN (17.5' KEY WEST) "Owning a boat isn't for everyone, so we decided to start small with a boat that was manageable and relatively maintenance free. This boat was our test run to see if boat ownership was for us."

THE EGG (9' DINGHY) "This is the tender for CYGNET II, which means 'little swan'."

THE GOOD LUFF (22.5' ENSIGN) "Craig and I purchased the 1972 boat in 1974. It had not been named. We agreed to each come up with some potential names. Craig held a cocktail party inviting a bunch of friends and we pulled the names out of a hat and voted. The overwhelming choice was submitted by my wife, Lesley."

THE JOY OF FREEDOM (24' NIMBLE) "Out of the love of the ocean and the freedom we have to enjoy it, through sailing her."

THE KRABBY PATTY (22' BOSTON WHALER OUTRAGE) "We purchased the boat used from a person in Maine. The boat was a little unkempt. Our children where young at the time and we asked them what to name the boat. Based on what they saw - and on one of their favorite TV shows of the time - they decided to name it after 'The Krabby Patty' from Sponge Bob Square Pants; Mr. Crab's hamburger combination. We contacted the TV show and obtained the correct 'font' which was invented for the show and is represented with the boats name/lettering."

THE LAST TYPHOON (19' CAPE DORY) "This Cape Dory Typhoon was the last Typhoon to be built by Cape Dory. This was the last Typhoon off the line in 1985 and the last Typhoon prior to

Cape Dory ceasing operations. Hence the name, 'THE LAST TYPHOON'."

THE RIDE (INFLATABLE DINGHY) "The name of the inflatable dinghy for Strega is 'The Ride', which was suggested by the senior citizen transportation that many cities provide. Keeping with the witch theme, the dinghy has a broom stick painted on both sides of the pontoons."

THE RIGHT STUFF (32' BRISTOL) "From the novel of the same name. I'm an airline pilot and I was trying to think of a meaningful aviation term to use for a name. In the book, the term 'right stuff', refers to the trait of certain pilots that allows them to excel or even recover from life threatening situations when all hope seems lost. The boat has lived up to her name on countless occasions."

THE ROCKMORE (140' WEST SHORE MARINE BUILT RESTAURANT) "After completing THE ROCKMORE (the main structure where the galley for the restaurant is), a bunch of friends and ourselves were sitting on her in the water. A big boat passed by and Peter said, 'Boy, it sure does rock more than I thought it would.' Hence, the name. People have complimented us on our clever play on words, using the old Rockmere Hotel…but we weren't as clever as they thought we were. It simply rocked more in the water."

THE RX-ONE (31' SEA RAY) "The perfect name for a pharmacist's boat, who lives and works in Marblehead."

THE SAIL LOFT (16.5' TOWN CLASS) "I have always wanted to be a sailmaker, being a sailor for most of my life. I was struggling with a 40' sailboat jib in my sail loft (read that as basement) and rationalized that a Town Class had sails small enough to fit into my loft, so acquired a Townie to use as a trial horse for my sails. As a consequence, I named the boat "the Sail Loft" for two reasons: I intended to use the boat as a trial horse for my sail making effort , and Maddie's used to be referred to as the "Sail Loft" because Ted Hood got started behind Maddie's.

My assumption was that I couldn't lose on either account and potentially I might be able to get Maddie's to sponsor the boat in the future.....imagine a Townie main with "Free Beer at Maddie's Sail Loft Tomorrow" in great red letters across the belly of the sail...what a hit. Oh, the sails, perhaps a close third."

THIMBLE BLADDER (12' COHASSET PRAM) "Named for the CT islands that the boat was built on."

3rd CENTURY (23' 1973 RAVEN) "The name comes from the fact that two of our friends own this classic boat. The first Century was a 1958 Resorter, the second Century was a 1972 Buccaneer, and ours is a 1973 Raven. I always felt it would have been more clever to name the boat after someone or something from the third century, like the plague, repeating crossbow or a Roman Emperor."

THISTLE (37' TARTAN) "Thistle is the national flower of Scotland."

THURSDAY'S CHILD (24' BRIDGES POINT) "My wife chose the name 30 years ago, for the famous nursery rhyme, '...Thursday's child has far to go'..."

TIBURON (25' GRADY WHITE) "We moved to Marblehead from Tiburon, CA where our 3 girls were born. Tiburon is a water town North of San Francisco. The name Tiburon derives from the Spanish word 'tiburon' which means 'shark'."

TIGGER TOO (28' ERICSON) "When my son Christopher was about 5 years old, I sold my first boat, 'Jedi', a Corinthian, and bought an Ericson 25. He liked 'Winnie the Pooh' stories at the time, so my wife and I decided to name the boat after a Pooh character. You can't name a boat 'Eyore' or 'Piglet', but 'Tigger' sounded good and the boat became 'Tigger'. When I moved up to an Ericson 28 five years later, we remembered that our son had enjoyed the book <u>Winnie the Pooh and Tigger Too</u>, so 'Tigger Too' (not 'Tigger II') she became."

TILLOO (23' PARKER) "Our boat is very similar, at least in our opinion, to boats that we chartered when on vacation in Abaco, Bahamas. There are many geographic landmarks down there that bear the Tilloo name. We named the boat after a favorite spot of ours called Tilloo Bank. The snorkeling is great and the water is shallow, making it easy to find great shells, sea biscuits and sand dollars. We have a big collection from there that we managed to pack well so there was minimal breakage! Many fond memories for the four of us."

TIME FLIES (21.9' SEACRAFT) "We are passionate fly fishermen and realize that time is fleeting--being with family and friends on the water makes time fly."

TIMELESS (58' HATTERAS) "Timeless became our home in the summer of 2013. We are living a life-long dream of living aboard. Timeless was the 2nd boat we looked at, and eventually purchased, and we loved the name so decided to keep it."

TINAVIRE (31'7" INTERNATIONAL 500) "The original 'TINAVIRE' was built in 1927 at Herreshoff's, designed by Sterling Burgess, and built for E. Root. The name was made up as follows: Navire means 'to swim' in Latin. Tinavire means to swim against the tide, or buck the current."

TIOGA TOO (44' POWER) "TIOGA in American Indian means beautiful maiden. It has now been in use on family sailboats for three generations."

TOM BOWEN'S CHURCH (20' AQUASPORT) "In the 1600's, the women and children were escorted from the town to the Ferry Landing on the Salem Harbor side, near the Green Street/Naugus Head area. While the women and children took the ferry to church in Salem, the men adjourned to a pub run by Tom Bowen. This was located high above the ferry landing on Naugus Head and called 'Tom Bowen's Church'. When the ferry returned to Marblehead, the men left Tom Bowen's to escort the women and children home."

TONTINE (36' C&C) "Joint partnership between my wife and me."

TOOTH & NAIL (30' CHAPARRAL SIGNATURE CRUISER) "I am a dentist, hence the 'tooth'. My husband is a contractor, real estate developer, hence the 'nail'."

TOPHER (37' TUGBOAT) "The name is taken from ChrisTOPHER."

TORCH (30' S2 9.1) "In 1984, eight identically equipped S2 9.1 Meters were selected for the inaugural Liberty Cup Regatta in New York Harbor celebrating the 100 anniversary of the Statue of Liberty. The boats were sailed by some of the most famous and successful sailors in the world, representing nations around the globe. Ted Turner, Gary Jobson and Harold Cudmore skippered crews full of America's Cup talent through several ties in this widely publicized, match-racing event. Boats were named with a Statue of Liberty theme including Torch, which is its original name."

TRIPLE PLAY (46' POST SPORT FISHERMAN) "This boat is the owner's third. The first two were called DELIVERANCE and STRIKE TWO."

TRIPLE PLAY (DYER DOW ROWBOAT) "To get out to our whaler from Stramski's we bought a used Dyer Dow rowboat that can really only hold three people in a fair sea. We named this 'Triple Play' due to its capacity of three people going out to play on the water."

TRIPOLI (22' MARSHALL CATBOAT) "'To the shores of Tripoli'. What better name for an old marine (USMC)."

TSUNAMI (27' MAKO) "Because of the wake it throws! We ski behind it."

TULLY-HO (21' GRADY WHITE) "We all live on Tully Road. We have become such good friends, we decided to by a boat together. We enjoy being together with our families.

Ellen has a sister who lives in Kentucky. Her husband advises horse breeders on nutrition. Since we all liked the name (we live on the same street) and family has ties to horse breeding – TULLY-HO! (Take off on 'Tally-Ho'!)"

TULLY MARS (23' REGULATOR) "Tully Mars (Tully) is a robin egg blue 23' Regulator center console which was named after the main character in Jimmy Buffet's book, A Salty Piece of Land.

As the story goes, I bought the boat sight unseen over the phone from a friend's brother while vacationing in Key Largo and reading Buffet's book. Never knew the color till it was unwrapped during the spring the following year. It took some getting used to but now it's well known among those fishing first light. As for the name, Tully Mars, is pretty much a can do anything guy from fly fishing for tarpon, flying airplanes and dating beautiful women. Everyman's dream and a great boat name."

TUMBLER (28' ALERION EXPRESS) "Although originally from Brooklyn, NY, my father had a burning desire to learn to sail. Soon after he and my mother were married, he bought a Lightning and taught himself to sail. Once he had the basics down, he moved up to a New Horizon, an International 500, and finally, a Morgan 38. The New Horizon came with the name 'Tumbler' and my father decided it was easier to keep it. Since the family name was 'Tate', a friend coined the phrase 'A Tumbler full of Tates', and the name stuck. The next two boats were also named Tumbler. My father loved to race and cruise.

When his sailing days were over and we were buying the Alerion, my husband asked him what name he would suggest. He said it would be nice to carry on the name Tumbler, so we did. Now we love it and keep it in his honor. We decided to paint it Marblehead Green and it was the first boat in the harbor with that color."

U——

UNREEL (20' AQUASPORT) "This boat was purchased specifically to fish for bluefish. While the owners haven't had great success catching 'the blues', they have enjoyed every minute of trying."

V——

VAROA (30' NONSUCH) "Our first boat was a Catamaran, so we wanted a Polynesian name. I had to go to the Widner Library at Harvard to find a Polynesian dictionary, but it wasn't until I got to the V's that I found a name I liked. It means 'ethereal spirit'."

VIGILANTE (34.5' J105) "Bernhardt Goetz, the New York subway vigilante, was in the news late 1984. My wife and I were going through the dictionary for names on a ski weekend, when a friend reading the newspaper asked, 'How about VIGILANTE?', and it stuck. I later sent her roses for a thank you."

VIJA (36' CAL) "Name of wife (Latvian)."

VIM (36.8' SABRE SPIRIT) "Sabre Yachts and Jim Taylor Yacht Design created the Spirit model to be a fast and extremely elegant daysailer / weekender to bring back the excitement and exhilaration we all felt when we first discovered the pastime of sailing. The name Vim tries to capture the design goal. The word 'Vim' refers to lively and energetic spirit and enthusiasm, all of which Sabre and Taylor definitely accomplished!"

VIRAGO (36' LITTLE HARBOR EXPRESS) "Virago loosely defined means 'Strong & Heroic Woman'. It is also the name of an offshore sailboat the owner once sailed on, and the name of several British war ships."

VOLUNTEER (26' FORTIER LAUNCH) "Name from the Weld Ship Plaque from the Weld Shipping Line in the late 1800's."

VOYAGER (34' C&C) "VOYAGER's name was created and selected at a crew party that was held in part, to come up with a name for the new boat. The name conveys adventure, exploration, limitless possibilities and class."

W ———

WAD-A-LEE (17' SHAMROCK) "When my Dad left this planet I knew it was my duty to keep the seafaring tradition alive. And, like a lot of kids who grew up sailing, I want nothing to do with it anymore. I opted for a low maintenance runabout that would fit on the mooring that had been originally occupied by our rowing dinghy. Given my ineptitude as a real boater, the only way to pay proper homage to my father's expertise was to come up with a witty name.

17 feet is not a lot of boat when there's a little chop and a couple of passengers on board – she's wet and handles a bit on the 'waddley' side. My father's mother was a Marbleheader's Marbleheader. A dedicated Public School teacher, rabble rouser, and a woman who was Woman's Lib before there was Woman's Lib. Her maiden name was Wadaleigh. Sailing with my Dad, I did learn a few things. When he'd yell 'hard-a-lee' I knew exactly what to do - get the hell out of the way. It's a phrase I heard a lot, but probably never really understood. Thus the Wad-A-Lee was christened. She sit's pretty on our mooring and is prone to break down. Just the way Chris Kent would want it."

WANDERING STAR (33' MORGAN) "From the song of the same name, sung by Lee Marvin in the movie 'Paint Your Wagon'."

WARLOCK (26' NONSUCH) "WARLOCK = a male witch. An advantage in racing."

WASAIL (30' PEARSON) "An English toast meaning 'cheers'!"

WATERLILY (26' CAPE DORY) "She is named after quite a beautiful 19th century wooden barge which cruised the canal system and the Thames River in England. We encountered her the year we purchased our own 'WATERLILY', as an exhibit in the Maritime Museum (the one designed by Sir Christopher Wren) in Greenwich, England. We decided to name our boat in her honor."

WATER RAT (22' AQUASPORT) "'Water Rat' is a southern California name for a person who loves boats and being on the water. (The owner is from southern California.)"

WAVE MAGIC (36' MACGREGOR CATAMARAN) "The original boat name was 'Mirror Image' and it was agreed that a new name would be taken as part of the sales agreement. I needed to match the 10" high x 6' long name letters that were painted on the gel coat and a faint image remained when the old name was removed. I wanted some name that would give a sense of how the boat moved effortlessly and cut through the waves at 1.5 times true wind speed. Then, it also seems that a boat that can go faster than the wind would be magic. AHA, the name 'Wave Magic' was born. This particular McGregor 36' catamaran that is hull #216 of 156 made, is followed all over the world, via my website, due to its customization and it is one of the few left in service that is in perfect condition."

WELLS CARGO (21' OCEANIC) "Our first son's name is Wells. For his first Christmas, he received a red wagon with the name 'WELLS CARGO' and we liked it!"

WHALE-PATH (30' J) "'Whale-Path' is an Anglo Saxon name for 'the sea'."

WHEELIE FAST (23' SEA LEGS AMPHIBIOUS RIB) "The boat was built in New Zealand and we bought it in 2011. It has wheels on the front and back which are used to propel it on land. When in the water, the wheels come up and the Evenrude outboard will run it at 40 knots. So the boat is Wheelie Fast!!!"

WHIP (30' ETCHELLS) "Since naming a boat can be extremely difficult, this owner resorted to using this colorful old Marblehead word to name most of his many racing boats. Shouting 'Whip' in a crowd has been known to illicit a response of 'Down Bucket' (another colorful Marblehead phrase) if another true Marbleheader is present."

WHIPLASH (20' AQUASPORT) "This is a play on words as the owners have 'whip' in their last name."

WHISPER (30' C&C) "The owner's daughter, Emily, said that the boat is so quiet that it sounds like a 'whisper'. Hence the name."

WHITE BUFFALO (25' CAPE DORY) "In Indian folklore, a 'white buffalo' is considered to be like a god."

WHITECAP (26' PEARSON) "Named after all the graduate nurses who wore whitecaps. Each nursing school had its own individual cap which was unique to their school, and identified the RN's who wore them with pride as graduates of a specific school.

The caps were phased out decades ago but are still remembered by the nurses who wore them."

WHITE WAVE (39'10" CONCORDIA YAWL) "Name from a book, White Wave, written by Diane Wolkstein and illustrated by Ed Young. This is a Chinese tale about a beautiful moon goddess, White Wave. Stars and moons are a well recognized Concordia symbol."

WHY NOT (12.5' BULLSEYE) "Came with the boat when purchased. Why Not?"

WILDCAT (13' BEETLECAT) "This boat was named by the previous owner, Joanne Wild. The name 'WILDCAT' is a play on words."

WILD GOOSE (20' BERTRAM) "Named by my father in Connecticut, where the boat lived from 1970-1986, when we brought it to Marblehead."

WINDFALL (26' SISU) "Having grown up with sailboats, my father and I decided when the 'wind falls', we should have a power boat."

WINGS (33.5' IOD) "There is a hymn that is titled 'Eagle's Wings', and since I enjoy the song, I felt this would be a proper name for our IOD. However, both Maura and Erin, my daughters, said, 'No Daddy. Name the boat just WINGS.' So the name was dictated to me by an eight year old and a six year old! And they say it's a man's world!"

WINGS OF THE MORNING (19' BUZZARDS BAY) "Name from Psalm 139 verse 9-10. 'If I take the wings of the morning and dwell in the uttermost parts of the sea, even there shall thy left hand lead me and thy right hand shall hold me.'"

WINSOME (24' KRAMER QUARTER TON) "WINSOME has been used earlier this century for a handsome, larger yacht (a schooner I believe) and probably for a 19th century yacht as well. Winsome is a lively, friendly, poised, self-confident, attractive young woman."

WIRED (30' ETCHELLS) "'We're wired' is an expression used by the crew when a racing sailboat is trimmed properly and is gaining ground on her competitors."

WITCHCRAFT (26' SPORTS FISHERMAN) "I work at the Salem Witch Museum."

WITCH CRAFT (INFLATABLE DINGHY) "The name of the inflatable dinghy for Sabrina is "Witch Craft" since we are never sure which boat we will use the dinghy for."

WOMBAT (20' AQUASPORT) "Where we bought the boat from, the owner had named all his boats after Australian marsupials."

WOODEND III (27' 1968 CHEOY LEE, NEWELL CADET) "Originally sold to Marbleheader Mary Sproule by Graves Yachts, Marblehead. We purchased her in Southwest Harbor, Maine. In 1995, we brought her home and kept her original name."

WOODWIND (34' HINCKLEY) "The name is a play on words."

WOODYA COULDYA (26' CENTER CONSOLE) "Being in the lumber business, I wanted to reference either lumber or wood in the name. My wife was reading Dr Seuss's Green Eggs and Ham and the sentence, 'Would ya could ya on a boat?' stuck."

WRECKLESS ABANDON (9' ZODIAC) "'I'm off with reckless abandon!' were the words of a seafaring friend every morning. So now, with a slightly patched, well used rubber duck, I enjoy the fun and exercise of rowing, and the pleasures of being on the water with RECKLESS ABANDON."

WYNDE SONG (32' 1974 ENDEAVOR CRUISING SLOOP) "The first (used) Firefly racing dinghy I purchased was named Windsong and aware of the possibility of bringing bad luck down on her by changing her name, I modified it to the 'Olde English' spelling Wynde and made it two words. I am of that heritage. She was an extremely successful little boat and I've named all of my succeeding boats, 5, the same."

WYNNER (19' CITATION) "As you can tell by the spelling, the name of the boat came from our last name."

Y———

YANKEE DOODLE (18' EASTERN) "The name was passed down from a previous power boat that was shared with our boating partners. The previous boat, an Aquasport, had the same name. I do not know the name's origin."

YEOMANETTE (31' TIARA) "In tribute to my maternal grandmother I named my boat Yeomanette, her rank in the Navy, World War I. We remember her patriotism, her strength and her zest for life."

YOU SEXY THING! (19' RHODES 19) "'You Sexy Thing' is a song featured in one of our favorite movies, the 1997 British comedy, 'The Full Monty'. The lyrics go like this, 'I believe in miracles, where you from, you sexy thing?'

Quite frequently when we go for a sail, someone in the other boat will enthusiastically exclaim, 'Hey, You Sexy Thing!' as we sail by them!"

Z ——

ZAP! (22' PEARSON ENSIGN) "'ZAP!' is a combination of the last names of the two owners. Most partnerships seem destined to fail during the first or second season. After all, just the right mesh of personalities and skills is critical to the longevity of such a relationship. In the fall of 1980, Emily Jane... and I decided that we both liked sailing enough to take the plunge and purchase Ensign #1144 from an attorney in New York City.

Between 1982 and 1988, we raced almost every weekend with the dwindling Ensign fleet in the Marblehead Racing Association. While I usually ended up at the helm, Emily provided navigational skills, organizational talent, and above all, good judgment in all situations. After the demise of Ensign racing in Marblehead in the late 80's, 'ZAP!' served us well as the great recreational boat that is the Ensign. The partnership easily could have lasted well into the 21st century, but Emily died of cancer at age 41 in June of 1993, after a courageous two-year battle. Thus, the partnership of 'ZAP!' came to a premature end, but not without enough good memories to last a lifetime."

ZEPHYR (30' CATALINA) "The boat got its name because 'zephyr' means wind and the owner's last name begins with a 'Z'."

*****

Abalash

allegro semplicita

Atlantic Wavedancer

BALEEN

MARBLEHEAD, MA

BANTRY

BLUE SIDE UP

CHANDELLE

CHENANGO

MARBLEHEAD, MA

CHRISTIAN MICHAEL

El Dorado
MARBLEHEAD, MA

EndorFin

ES-CAP-E
MARBLEHEAD, MA

Fall **❋* *Line

fandango
MARBLEHEAD, MASS.

FAR NIENTE

FIREWOOD

FLY BY

GEMINI
MARBLEHEAD, MA

Good Question

GOTSCH'A

GRADY-WHITE

IMUS MCHUGH
MARBLEHEAD

INDRA

Inisfail
MARBLEHEAD

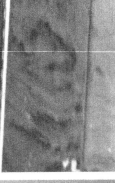

Invigorator

EUGENE T. CONNOLLY

NIXIE

Sunfisch

Khoka Moya

ISLANDER
MARBLEHEAD, MA

JOLI II

Katabatic

KNOTLESS

M. JULIP

MACKINAW
MARBLEHEAD

mo chuísle

PLEIONE
MARBLEHEAD

RECON ★ MISSION

RIVAL

MARBLEHEAD, MA

ROCK STAR

MARBLEHEAD, MA

SHALLOW UP

MARBLEHEAD

SIROCCO

MARBLEHEAD, MA

Starry Night

MARBLEHEAD

START ME UP

Suerte · Verde

SUMMER SCHOOL
Marblehead, MA

Sunshine Daydream
MARBLEHEAD, MA

TAYGETA
MARBLEHEAD

THE KRABBY PATTY
Marblehead, MA

Tilloo

TIMELESS
NORTH CONWAY, NH

TINAVIRE
MARBLEHEAD

"All of us have in our veins the exact same percentage of salt in our blood that exists in the ocean, and, therefore, we have salt in our blood, in our sweat, in our tears. We are tied to the ocean. And when we go back to the sea - whether it is to sail or to watch it - we are going back from whence we came."

-John F. Kennedy

CPSIA information can be obtained at www.ICGtesting.com
Printed in the USA
LVOW03s2149071214

417697LV00018B/299/P

9 780964 101319